Praise for
Driven to Succeed

"This is the inspiring true story of how a kid from the Rez became a business leader and successful motivational speaker. Learn to change your life for the better from someone who has done it himself — Kendal Netmaker!"

Wab Kinew, #1 Bestselling Author of *The Reason You Walk*

"Kendal knows what it takes to become successful. He captivates the reader through his personal journey and shares valuable insight on what it takes to persevere."

Michael Linklater, Canada's #1 FIBA 3X3 Basketball Player

"An unadulterated look at the many trials and tribulations facing our Indigenous youth here in Canada. Kendal's story is one of perseverance and bravery; of overcoming societal hurdles and becoming the person you want to be despite the manufactured social constraints that we place upon one another. A compelling tale told with the passion and grit of a genuine artist. Truly, an inspiring read."

JP Gladu, President and CEO of the Canadian Council for Aboriginal Business

"This inspiring and motivational book opens your mind and heart to the unlimited potential that resides within you. It can change your life!"

Brian Tracy, Author, Speaker, Consultant

"Kendal's story will inspire and motivate you to achieve your own success using his 5 steps to get you from where you are to where you want to be!"

Chris Widener, Bestselling Author of *The Art of Influence*

"Kendal is a stellar person. I've had the pleasure of speaking with him, and I love how he remains humble and hungry to give back despite his success. *Driven to Succeed* is one of the best books I've seen on how people can set goals and achieve them."

Manu Goswami, Canada's Top 20 Under 20 and Young Entrepreneur of the Year

"Be careful with this book. Kendal's inspirational story of defying the odds to overcome enormous challenges will compel you to achieve more."

Paul Martin, Author, Coach and Mentor

"Kendal's story is most inspiring as it demonstrates his incredible perseverance through adversity. With a "never quit" mentality, he has achieved what many only dream about."

Denis Prud'homme, Serial Entrepreneur and Mentor

"Kendal's remarkable journey is peppered with personal wisdom and profound insights. His simple yet powerful formula for success makes you realize that no obstacle is too big to overcome."

Allan Kehler, Bestselling Author and Motivational Speaker

"Kendal is definitely a person who shines in my eyes. He's been through hell himself and has shown how he didn't let adversity get the best of him. I can highly attest that Kendal can help you drive to the success you've yearning for."

Tofe Evans, Ultra-endurance Athlete, Resilience
Thought Leader, Bestselling Author

"Kendal's story is a must read for all people — young and old, Indigenous or not. It shows what a bit of luck, lots of hard work and dedicated effort and a clear focus on the goal can mean to a person. There are few who have inspired so many others as Kendal, and this book will surely add to that number."

Steve McLellan, CEO of the
Saskatchewan Chamber of Commerce

"A book like this takes guts to write. Real, vulnerable, and honest to the degree that people need to hear to really understand what Kendal has overcome and how they can achieve their own greatness. A must-read for those who are looking for a little bit of inspiration and the tactics and guidance on how to get to where they want to go."

Eric Termuende, Bestselling Author of *Rethink Work*

"Kendal's story is such an inspiration. Rising from his circumstances to build a successful company and then to teach others how to do the same for themselves.... it's an awesome gift. One that will keep on giving for generations to come."

Jane Atkinson, Author of *The Wealthy Speaker 2.0*
and *The Epic Keynote*

"Kendal's story not only demonstrates how he harnessed his talents to turn difficult situations into inspirational outcomes, but you will finish this book being inspired to do the same. His ability to overcome challenges to achieve greatness gives hope to all of us who must face difficult situations both at home and at work."

Michael Salone, CEO of 3-6TY and Author of *Tagging for Talent: The Hidden Power of Social Recognition in the Workplace*

"I have followed Kendal's entrepreneurial adventures for many years. He is truly a role model for First Nation's — and frankly all — entrepreneurs. He is on a mission to help others in life and business. This book shows you the way — the Kendal way."

W. Brett Wilson, Entrepreneur and Philanthropist

"If you think that entrepreneurship or another goal is out of your reach, this inspiring book is for you. Kendal Netmaker shares his own obstacle-filled journey, as well as his realistic advice on how to create your own business and achieve your dreams."

Julia Deans, CEO, Futurpreneur Canada

"Having worked with a number of Indigenous communities, I have seen how important it is to have role models like Kendal. It takes courage to share the personal stories of one's life. Kendal's story will inspire you and show you that if you stay driven, you too can succeed."

Joel Pederson, Founder of Fitness 2J2, retired Police Officer

"It is difficult to quantify how astonishing Mr. Netmaker's success is without context. In life, some people get to start on third base; Kendal wasn't even on the team. Read critically, this book is full of lessons necessary to success."

Dallas Soonias, First Indigenous Male to
Play Team Canada Volleyball

"I believe there are any number of people who can benefit from Kendal's book, it hit me where I live, our lives are very much alike. We were both raised by our mother and grandmother. We both came from poverty. If Kendal and I can win Big you can too and Kendal has done a Wonderful job of showing you how in the following pages. Get two copies and give one to a friend and then share the path to Success Kendal has created for you with you friend."

Bob Proctor, From the movie "The Secret"
and Author *You Were Born Rich*

"Kendal is a true inspiration. This book speaks to the resilient, passionate and incredible man he is. A true example that anything is possible."

Brigette Lacquette, Team Canada Women's
Hockey Olympic Silver Medalist

DRIVEN TO
SUCCEED

FROM POVERTY
TO PODIUM

Kendal Netmaker

Made for Success
PUBLISHING

Made for Success Publishing
P.O. Box 1775
Issaquah, WA 98027

If you are seeking to purchase this book in quantity for sales
promotion or corporate use, please contact Made for Success at 425-
657-0300 or email Sales@MadeforSuccess.net. Your local bookstore
can also help you with discounted bulk purchase options.

ISBN 978-1-64146-323-2 (Physical Book)
ISBN: 978-1-64146-333-1 (Audiobook)
ISBN: 978-1-64146-334-8 (eBook)
LCCN: 2018904336

Library of Congress Cataloging-in-Publication data

Netmaker, Kendal
Driven to Succeed: From Poverty to Podium
"A First Nation Success Story"
pages. Cm
1. Business & Money > Management & Leadership > Motivational
2. Biographies & Memoirs > Ethnic & National > Native American
3. Self-Help > Success

Printed in Canada

CONTENTS

INTRODUCTION

Before My Time

REGARDLESS OF WHAT you have gone through in your life, you can always change it. Your circumstances do not determine who you can become. If you woke up alone tomorrow without any material possessions, you would be left with two things. One: your gifts – that which make you the awesome person that you are; and two: the story you have that has the power to impact thousands of people in your lifetime. I wrote this book to help those who have had to overcome many obstacles in their lifetime and I have given you tools that will help you along in your own journey.

Driven to Succeed begins with my mom and grandmother, two women who sacrificed so much for myself and my sisters, while raising us alone on a Reservation, surrounded by poverty and sometimes violence. Most of what I will share with you has come from women. This is my mom's story:

"Many of us have our very own story to tell, many of us have our own family dynamics. My Mother Emma was a fluent Cree speaker and that is all she spoke to us. She also took part in cultural ceremonies and taught us the importance of our Culture and Traditions. In the end it seemed that she lived her life for her children, grandchildren and her parents. There was hardly a day that went by that she did not visit her late parents. She worked hard to feed and clothe us. She rarely ever had the means of an income. There were no luxuries such as a washer/dryer or a wood heater; water had to be hauled. Everything was manual labor. In time, latter years, we had a fridge, a black and white TV, and a wringer washer. We grew up materialistically poor, but we were rich with togetherness and love from my mother (and grandparents), and also from my father for the short time he was here on earth.

My Dad was a fluent Plains Cree Speaker and also spoke English. He was a jolly, friendly and kind man who loved to play soccer and played it very well. I recall our family going to our reserve sports grounds, where there were many sporting events. These are good memories for me. In time, however, my Dad became an alcoholic – and it took its toll on him. My Dad used to try to sustain a living for us. He passed away at the early age of 49.

The last five years of my Mother's life were hard on her; she used a wheelchair due in part to her diabetes, but she didn't let it stop her from being a hard worker. She still worked hard and continued to move about each day, even though she wasn't a healthy woman. She passed away at the age of 79. We were blessed and very lucky to have had our mother as long as she could be here on earth. I loved my mother so much. I had seen how hard she worked to feed and clothe us and suffer and sacrifice for us. I tried to give her dignity by being there for her when she needed me in the latter part of her life.

My children's Dad and I did not have a healthy relationship; we argued a lot. It wasn't as happy as I hoped it would be. The burden of responsibilities and the lack of steady income became overwhelming. I wasn't employed; I stayed home with my children.

When he fractured my nose that one year, I thought: *he's mistreated me many times and now he's going to start hitting me? I don't think so.* That's when I knew that I had to leave. As difficult as it was, my children were more important to me than trying to keep a husband. I knew things weren't going to get any better for us. I reported that incident to the authorities; I filed my report; but when court time came a few months later, his story seemed more plausible than mine. This perception influenced the judge's decision to give him no jail time and only give him a minor fine; for this reason I lived in fear for almost two decades. The system failed me as an Indigenous Women. I decided to leave at an opportune time, when he was away for a weekend.

We then relocated to Saskatoon; I was thinking I could raise the children there and look for opportunities for myself. We briefly stayed at an Interval House for Women and then transferred to North Battleford, but ultimately ended up moving to my home reserve. We moved in with my (late) Mother, for about six months, and then we moved into a house on the reserve when my cousin relocated.

And even though my four kids and I lived in a two-bedroom house, it was all we had. That is where I brought up my kids. I was very lucky to have had a mother that was there for us; otherwise I don't know what would've happened. Her support was a great source of strength; her love for her children and grandchildren was enormous.

I am just so grateful, Ninanaskomon, for everything. I am grateful that my late mother managed to avoid a crucial touchstone that has damaged the lives of so many people raised on reservations, namely attending Residential School. My Father, however, was not as lucky, and did attend Residential School. What is Residential School? Between 1831 and 1996, residential schools operated in Canada through arrangements between the Government of Canada and the church. One common objective defined this period – the assimilation of Aboriginal children. The children that attended experienced every type of abuse and thousands lost their lives.

It's been said that: 'We are all here for a reason.' It's just that sometimes it takes some of us a long time to understand and fully realize what that reason is.

Ninanaskomon (I am grateful)."

Inez Weenie (My Mom)

IT MAY NOT BE YOUR FAULT, BUT YOU CAN CHANGE IT!

Early Childhood

My name is Kendal Charles Netmaker. I was born April 27, 1987 in North Battleford, Saskatchewan, Canada, twenty minutes away from my reservation, Sweetgrass First Nation. As an infant my mother was told by an East Indian Doctor that: "This one is going to be a smart boy." She asked him how he knew but the Dr. wouldn't tell her. My mother would tell me this story in my early 20s, when she sensed that I might be steering in a negative path.

I am the oldest and have three younger sisters; my mother Inez raised us. From as early as I can remember, we lived in Big River First Nation. My dad is an amazingly fluent Cree speaker and I wish he could have taught me what he knows. Unfortunately, like many First Nations fathers at the time, my dad didn't know how to show love or affection. He led himself down an unhealthy path which involved drugs and alcohol. I don't remember seeing my dad too often on the reservation, but I do remember times where he would show us love and affection – something I will always cherish. There were times he would take us to the store to get treats with my sisters or pull us around on the sled in the winter, but these are only fond memories. In Kindergarten, I attended the local school called See See Wa Hum and I remember having an amazing teacher who showed me she cared about me and my other friends. She would often send me positive notes of encouragement, which motivated me to continue to try hard even though it was only Kindergarten. As I continued going to Kindergarten, I would see my father less and less. The times that he was around, my parents would argue to the point where my sisters and I would have to run out of the room. My mother's main focus was keeping us safe, but one day things got out of hand; I noticed my mom had a cast on her nose, of course, I was too young to figure out what had happened.

I remember my first life changing moment. It was a sunny afternoon on the rez and school was wrapped up for the year. I had just finished visiting cousins and was walking home. As I walked towards my house, I saw a truck parked outside of the house that belonged to my mom's best friend Audrey. I also saw my mother loading our family's belongings in garbage bags and boxes into the truck. As I approached the house, my mother stopped what she was doing and looked at me. "Start packing your bag," she said. "We don't have much time." I nodded and raced inside the house. I looked around and tried to see what I could use to pack my belongings in; all I had in my possession was a little Ninja Turtles backpack and I began packing as many toys as I could fit in it.

That was the day my mother left my dad. After that, we found ourselves staying in various Interval Houses. These were women's shelters for single mothers who had nowhere to go with their children. We didn't have a place to call home. I remember shelters where we would often only spend one to two weeks at most. I remember it like it was yesterday – playing with toys at the shelters and wondering when we were going to go back home. My mom was trying to find a way to look after us four children by herself and I cannot imagine what she had to go through to make that happen.

Another time we were living in an apartment in Prince Albert, Saskatchewan and I began acting out. One day I decided I was old enough to go hang out with a crowd of kids and took off to a local park without telling my mom. She panicked, like any caring parent would. My younger sister Kendra and my mom went looking for me and found me a few blocks away hanging with other kids (I later realized they were neglected) and disciplined me the whole way home. My mom had to leave my infant sister Farrah sleeping in her crib just so she could catch up to where I was. I was a handful, but my mom made sure I wasn't hanging with the wrong crowds at a young age. Like any kid, I was often mad at her when I felt like she wasn't letting me do what I wanted to do, or be as free as my friends were growing up. But I later found out that most kids who were allowed to do what they wanted, ended up not going very far in life; lesson learned.

Over time we bounced around women's shelters and apartments in Prince Albert, Saskatoon and North Battleford, as my parents got back together and broke up again several times. When my mom was 7.5 months pregnant with my younger sister Kendra, she broke her arm and was unable to carry me or look after me properly. My Kokum (my grandma) moved in with us for six months to watch over me (apparently I used to make her watch me sing Elvis songs until I was all sweaty from the big performance). My Kokum's involvement in my upbringing would be instrumental to my teen and adult years because I learned so many values from her. From an early age, I learned to respect elders and the first one was my Kokum.

Grade 1-2

When I was 6 years old, we moved in with my Kokum at her house in Sweetgrass First Nation. My Kokum had taught me many valuable lessons in my life through her actions. She didn't speak fluent English and we had difficult times communicating, because I am not a fluent Cree speaker. She had taken us in to her two-bedroom house, and for a long time we had no personal space, but it very warm and welcoming and I loved the presence of my Kokum. She was the best cook and always made amazing bannock and soup for us. My Kokum loved to spoil her grandchildren with chocolate treats. I remember one time where she pretended to be the tooth fairy and had left her "bingo change" in an envelope for me in the morning under my pillow. I was definitely excited to buy junk food the next day.

It is not easy to find housing on a First Nations Reservation in Canada. We cannot legally own our own homes and in my community, there was no economic development and job creation. If you were lucky to find a way to obtain a vehicle, the closest city was North Battleford, approximately 25 minutes away by car. We finally got lucky when my mother's cousin moved out of a small, two-bedroom house not far from my Kokum's house, and we were able to move into it. To have our own home after years of moving about was amazing; we were thrilled. We immediately began to move our belongings into our new home.

I was the spoiled kid in my family because I was the only one to have my own room; my three younger sisters had to share the other room and many times my mom slept on the couch, until I graduated high school. This was just one of the many sacrifices my mom made for us. Through our culture, *respect* between male/female siblings was very high and I was not allowed to speak inappropriately around them or wrestle with them. This was part of our teachings.

I would spend most of my time playing outside making forts, playing sports and just being a kid. Later on, I was grateful to obtain a Nintendo Game. But the game didn't stay in our house all the time; quite often, it would make its way to the local pawnshop so we could have groceries for a few weeks; then when child tax payments and/or welfare was issued, I would get my game out from the pawn shop for a few more weeks, and the cycle continued. Collecting and getting change for empty cans and bottles became a lifestyle many of us got used to. I believe that we grew up in a system that conditioned us into depending on the government/First Nations Communities to help us get ahead in life, because we had laws that secluded us and that didn't allow us to create our own income and opportunities like mainstream society. You pair that with the effects of Residential Schools and it becomes a disaster. As I would later educate myself, I came to realize that we can also unlearn conditioned behavior by replacing it with a new one. We just have to be willing to educate ourselves and work towards a new habit.

There are certain business models that prey on people in poverty such as: "Cash your checks for fast cash," "Get a vehicle today with no money down," "Get this living room set with no money down!" I could go on and on. These businesses (I don't even want to call them that) do nothing but put people who are vulnerable into debt; it becomes nearly impossible to get ahead, due to the outrageous interest rates where some people end up paying for things as much as 3 or 4 times the actual original price. We would spend the rest of my youth battling the pawnshop effect with our bicycles, televisions, games, etc. just to put food on the table.

I remember when my mom came home with a brand new 13" color TV. It felt like we had a giant 50" plasma television that day; I was so grateful. We put that TV on top of an old school wooden box TV that had been broken for years. When you don't grow up with a lot of material possessions, and when you are blessed with something new, you appreciate it more.

I grew up around females my whole life and didn't have male relatives close by to play sports with. I would often have to force my sister Kendra to play outside with me. We were both talented in many sports and soccer was the one we started to play more and more outside in our spare time. Sports would inevitably make our brother and sister bond strong in our later years.

Growing up in Sweetgrass, I was introduced to traditional ceremonies and most summers my mom would be participating in them. At that age, I was only playing around the camp and did not understand what was taking place each summer. Throughout the year there would be other cultural events that we would attend as a family. As I attended these, I was forced to learn other keys that would help me in my adult years. One of the most profound was to "listen more than you speak," and I learned this by attending cultural ceremonies and watching elders and how they conducted themselves. They rarely spoke and when they did, it was always profound and had impact. They had a great respect for the cultural ceremonies they were conducting for the community and I learned to respect and listen from them.

Every summer my dad would pick myself and my 3 younger sisters up and we would go visit at his house on Big River First Nation. I was always excited to go visit because

I would get a chance to hang out with my dad and other relatives. My Moshum (my father's dad) was a cattle farmer and I remember when we would go and visit and he would always be working outside. My Kokum (my father's mom) would also be outside skinning or smoking moose or other wild meat for the family to eat later. They were hard workers and I was grateful for the visits we had with them. My dad would later inherit the farm and continue the work his father left for him after our Moshum passed away.

Like with many Indigenous families, alcohol was a problem for us. As I got older, and we visited more often, I would witness many of my family members drinking and partying while kids were around. I know this because I was at those parties during several of the times we visited my dad and my grandparents. They would tell me not to drink when I got older. I could tell they were hurting but I was just a kid. I am not sure what might have happened if I continued to grow up in an environment like that, but I know I wouldn't be in a good situation today.

I remember one time while visiting, my cousin Shawn and I were playing a card game. We both had a few bucks in our pockets and decided to gamble and whoever got all the money won. After several games, I was the lucky winner and had won all the money; I was excited. When he went home, I felt immediate guilt and I wanted to give him his money back. So I began to dig a hole near a tree and put his money in there. The following summer when we came back to visit, we both dug up the mound and I gave him his money back.

It bothered me taking his money because I already knew what it was like to not have much.

Back on Sweetgrass one day I had a 'genius' idea of how to make some cash to buy some junk food from the local store. I knew that I had a Nintendo N64, toys and a silly kid imagination, so I immediately began to construct an amusement part in my bedroom. When I was all done, I began to charge my sisters a nickel to a dime per 15 minutes of playing time on my Nintendo or to throw a ball into a hoop to win one of my toys. I had 4 to 5 games laid out and I started to see their nickels and dimes build after a few hours. After that, I felt guilty once again for taking their money and I gave it all back.

I developed empathy by watching how much my mom sacrificed for us. She would often have to pay $20 to $40 to someone just to take her grocery shopping to feed us. She always paid more than other people so she could be taken as a priority on the social assistance she was given each month. I decided at an early age that when I got older I was not going to rely on anyone but myself to get things done.

Living on the rez was very quiet and we didn't have a vehicle to take us on adventures. So I was forced to use my imagination and creativity. I would take old toys that didn't work and play with the motors until I eventually began to build gadgets out of nothing. I remember being able to build an airplane out of a 'pizza pop' card board, old motors and spare toy parts with a propeller that would almost move the plane. I also remember building a hockey net and a soccer net outside with spare wood parts we found in the bush. As a kid, my goal was to one day play hockey. My dad loved hockey and so did I. There was one big problem – our reservation didn't have an indoor or outdoor skating rink. I remember wanting to play hockey so badly that I would fill a 2-liter Pepsi bottle full of water and take it outside to pour on the road and let it freeze. After about 50 trips back and forth, I would have just enough of an ice patch to skate in a little circle and attempt to play hockey. But that didn't work out too well.

From a young age living in that house, I felt destined for big things. I had no idea what they were; I just believed that I could do something great. I used to hold a picture of myself living in the future wearing a black and white business suit; I had no idea it would eventually lead me here. I believe everyone has a feeling of what they want out of their life, some of us just lose that belief over time.

When I was in second grade attending Sweetgrass Elementary School, I would often get off the bus with a face and eyes red from crying. My mother later found out that I would get bullied a lot on the bus and even during school. I was a very small, "skinny" (I don't like that word), kid growing up and did not know how to defend myself. This led to my mom making a decision to put me in a different school.

But in the new school, the bullying didn't stop and would return many times throughout my later high school years. As I got older, I excelled in various sports but still got bullied; people would call me "chicken legs," "skinny," "string bean," and other names. The truth is, those words hurt in the moment and eventually led to me giving up basketball in grade 10 because I was too self-conscious of how "skinny" I was.

Words have power; you can use them to bring people up or bring them down. There are millions of people who suffer from low self-confidence and self-esteem. The words you choose to use on a friend, family member or stranger can help build them up or it can even trigger a devastating decision to take their own life one day. Choose to bring people up and you will have many friends that will do the same for you.

HOW ONE PERSON CAN CHANGE THE WORLD

Grade 3-9

FOR THE FIRST time in my life I was truly outside of my "comfort zone" at 8 years old when I first got off the bus to attend Cut Knife Elementary School. The town of Cut Knife was primarily a farming community also surrounded by neighboring First Nations Reservations that included Sweetgrass First Nation, Poundmaker First Nation and Little Pine First Nation. I knew right away that I was different primarily because I had an accent and darker skin than most of the other students. I knew I had to find a way to fit in with the farm kids. For the first few days I was a loner and during classes and recesses I would study how the kids would talk to each other and what they would talk about. This was the first time I was also forced to "adapt" to a new situation.

On the third day of school I approached several kids on the playground and began to ask them odd questions that they were interested in such as, "Hey how are your crops doing" or "How much rain did you get last night?" I really had no idea what I was even talking about. I was doing everything I could to adapt to them and build a connection. Some of the kids didn't want to talk to me but there were some who let me play with them. As I continued to make more connections, I would eventually start playing soccer with them at recess.

Athletic ability was one of my gifts; I was able to use it to quickly fit in to the soccer games they had each recess. Over time, I began to develop a great love for Soccer. The game gave me confidence and the more I practiced, the better I got. I just wished I could play on a real team. I would practice at home outside with my sister with the soccer net we built. After school and on weekends, all of my cousins and relatives would meet up at my Kokum's house to have a game of soccer. These were the best of times because my Kokum loved watching us play in her yard together. We would spend most weekends and many days during the week at my Kokum's house, which was within walking distance.

On the rez, we had to battle things that most people in Canada didn't have to worry about. For years, the running water would turn brown in our house and would not be safe to drink. However, what else were we supposed to drink? Most homes I would visit on the rez had major issues that would definitely not be safe in a city such as: structural issues, plumbing/leaks and mold, among others. This was all very normal to us growing up. As long as we had a roof over our heads, we were blessed. Most people on the rez were malnourished due to a lack of knowledge about how unhealthy their diets were. I grew up on macaroni and cheese, soup and bannock, pizza, pops and noodles – foods that delivered few beneficial nutrients. But it wasn't entirely my fault – the local store had no locally grown vegetables or fruits. When people consume empty calories (processed foods), the brain does not get nourished and continues to feel hungry until it gets the proper vitamins/minerals. Inevitably, Diabetes is a major problem that many of my relatives have had to battle. Unfortunately, First Nations people have some of the highest rates of diabetes in Canada due to lack of access to proper nutrition and clean drinking water.

Adapting to other people can also have its disadvantages. In grade 5, I remember failing numerous tests just to get a funny reaction from the kids in my class. This poor behavior would eventually send me to summer school and an extra reading program. But grade 5 was also the year that would change my life. It was the year I had become great friends with Johann, a boy from South Africa. Johann and I became close at recess playing soccer with the other kids. Out of the entire school, he was the only one to ask me, "Kendal, why aren't you playing soccer on the after school team? We go to neighboring towns like Wilkie, Marsden and Unity. You are just as good as any of us, why aren't you playing?" There was an awkward pause as I struggled to explain to Johann: "We don't have a vehicle, my only transportation is the bus to and from school, I don't have $50 to pay the fee, I don't even have soccer gear to play in, and my family is living on welfare." This was definitely something that Johann was not used to hearing. That very night he told his parents what I had told him at recess. And the next day, Johann's parents paid for me to play on the after school team; they would eventually drive me to my reserve after each game. They gave me my first opportunity to play organized sports with a coach, and that is something I am truly grateful for.

Johann and I became best friends and I would try to be at his house every weekend. They had a beautiful house at Attons Lake, SK. His mom was an amazing cook and cared deeply for everyone in her household – and her guests. I always felt welcomed when I would visit. His dad would become one of my biggest role models as a youth. Johann's family was originally from South Africa; his father brought his family to Canada when Johann was a child and became a doctor in pursuit of a brighter future in Canada. Johann's parents knew what it was like to start from nothing and struggle to build a better life. I believe he saw something good in me that allowed me to spend many days at his house over the next few years. His father had an insane work ethic. I used to watch him work, study, be an amazing father and husband all while leading a healthy lifestyle. He would run marathons around the lake (at least it felt like a marathon) while Johann and I would ride our bikes behind him follow-ing. He was a great role model and he would compliment me and encourage me in a positive way whether it was about a soccer game or how I was dressed that day. He gave me confidence when I couldn't find it in myself yet. Words have

power; you never know who you can impact by compliment-
ing another person.

By the time we were in seventh grade, I received some sad
news. Johann and his family were going to move a few hours
away to Saskatoon. I was devastated and wondered how I was
going to continue to play the game that I loved so much and
lose having my best friend at the same school. But what happened next changed not only my life, but that of my whole
family. Before they moved away, they gave me and my family a gift. It was something that was sitting in their drive-
way that they were not using – a 1986 Ford Crown Victoria.
They gave us a vehicle because they felt that my mom was
doing everything she could to help us grow into a brighter
future and they knew a car was what was needed to allow us
to continue playing after school sports. We couldn't believe
their generosity; we soon found my mom driving us to soccer
practices and becoming more involved in after school activi-
ties. Most of my farmer friends had nice cars and trucks and
while most people would feel uncomfortable with an older,
big vehicle pulling up after soccer practice, I was just grateful
to have a vehicle.

I would continue to visit Johann and his family when I
would have dentist appointments in Saskatoon – because in
grade 7, I also got braces, which would last for three years
(ouch). I remember like yesterday getting the braces on and
I was the only First Nations kid in the orthodontist chair
when an older "Caucasian women" was assigned to me. I
immediately sensed that she was discouraged to have me as

a patient. She cut my gums so badly and yanked my mouth around like a rag doll; I knew it had to do with the color of my skin because she treated all her other patients besides me with more respect. Racism would be a problem I would continue to face in some doctors' offices, stores and from strangers over the years.

Back at Cut Knife, there would be events that made people from my background very uncomfortable. Throughout the year there would be several potlucks, where each student was assigned a food item on the menu to bring to a school meal. Every single time I was assigned an item, I was unable to bring it, because we didn't have the extra money to do so. So you can imagine how haunting it was to show up to the potluck and have the kids mock you for not showing up with the food you were supposed to bring. It was embarrassing.

As we grew up, I also noticed that my fellow brothers and sisters from the neighboring First Nations Reservations were predominantly put into "Resource Rooms," where students who were basically not up to par with everyone else were sent to learn. They were secluded from everyone and I used to wonder how this was a better learning situation for them; it made no sense. I was one of the lucky ones who didn't get sent to that room. I believe this happened because I was able to adapt and fit in with my "white friends," which convinced my teachers that I was normal enough to be in a regular classroom. Later on in life, a boy from my rez who had been placed in one of the isolated learning rooms ended up committing suicide.

One day during 7th grade, we were all required to participate in a science fair. Our teacher insisted that we all needed to dress up sharp, which meant guys would have to wear dress pants, a dress shirt and a tie – none of which I owned. I had some money that I was saving in my room and I asked my mom if I had enough to buy a cheap outfit for the science fair. My mom measured me and we began to search through the Sears Catalogue. I was able to afford an outfit that I ordered in time for the Science Fair. The day of the science fair I was excited to be dressed up for the first time and ready to present my project (although it had nothing to do with science – it was about violence in video games). When I got to school my classmates told me to tuck my shirt in (I had no clue), and I had to ask our vice principal to tie my Mickey Mouse tie. After all that was done, I was dressed for success and I felt like a million bucks! I felt confident and was able to do my presentation on my own (even though I had a partner who skipped out). That day I got an honorable mention, which I was super proud of. I believe because I dressed the part, it elevated my confidence and I was able to give the presentation everything I had.

I am very grateful to the many people from Cut Knife and the surrounding area who allowed me to be their friend and allowed me into their homes. Several of my friends would invite me to camp over for a weekend and hang out. I would always be in awe of their homes and the stuff that they had. One in particular had a beautiful home, everything you would want in a house and even the breakfast his mom made was like something out of a movie.

Between grades 7 and 9, I started to play more sports – like volleyball and badminton. I grew fonder of the sport of volleyball primarily because I had great role models back home who always played it such as my mom, aunty, uncles, and cousins. We would play over old swing sets and eventually found a way to get a volleyball net in my Kokum's yard where we would meet up to have games after school. This was the beginning of my volleyball career.

In grade 9, I was playing a lot of floor hockey; there was an upcoming tournament in Wilkie, SK, and I decided to attend. During the tournament I was giving it everything I had when out of nowhere I saw my dad on the sidelines. He looked at me and said: "play hard son." I was shocked to see him there cheering me on; he later took me to North Battleford to eat and then dropped me off back at home. I knew how passionate he was about the game of hockey, I just wished there was a way for me to play ice hockey so he would make more time to come and see me. My dad loved hockey and he made time to go watch more hockey games than come and visit us as kids. Another time he picked me up to go golfing at Attons Lake. It was the fastest round of golf I had ever played because my dad was a very impatient player, but I was grateful for the opportunity nonetheless because I loved any chance to spend time with my dad. Spending time with my father was something my sisters and I craved more than anything as kids. We would get to see him a few times a year and each time we did, we were grateful.

At the end of grade 9, I decided it was time for me to

change schools, because I wanted to play on more developed sports teams, so I had to say goodbye to many of my friends I had made over the years and journey on to a new high school in North Battleford, Saskatchewan.

HOW LEADERS INFLUENCE THEIR TEAM

Grade 10-12

I ATTENDED MY remaining high school years at John Paul II Collegiate in North Battleford – a big change from Cut Knife, with many kids from the city and surrounding communities. I also noticed more First Nations students attending the school, which made me feel more comfortable. From day one, I had one intention: to play soccer and volleyball. I saw that the volleyball tryouts were the evening of my first day at school, and I decided to give it a shot. When I walked into the room I was immediately intimidated – the most I had ever been in my life – as everyone was screaming at the top of their lungs and there I was this shy kid from the rez who was hoping to make the team. I was thinking so negatively during the whole tryout, saying to myself *why are you here*

Kendal? You know you have no shot of making this team or *no one knows you here, you don't have a chance, just quit now.* I had convinced myself in my mind that I wasn't good enough and at the end of the practice I grabbed my backpack and rushed toward the door. I was about to leave when I heard a voice call my name. The person calling me was Doug Sieben, the volleyball coach and Physics teacher. He said, "Kendal, come on over here, I want to talk to you for a second." I walked over to him and he leaned in close and said: "Kendal, I really like what I saw today. You have a lot of potential. You might not get a lot of playing time this year, but I want you to be on my team. I see a lot of potential in you." That short conversation changed my life. For the first time, other than Johann's dad in elementary, someone I didn't even know yet was saying that he saw potential in me. The feeling of another male figure telling me that he saw potential in me gave me confidence, and I committed myself to his team until I graduated high school; Doug became my mentor, teacher and volleyball coach.

In grade 10, I was a very skinny kid and my self-esteem would take a hit after every comment made by kids in school about how skinny I was. But I was gifted athletically in most sports. Even in junior high, I would win free throw competitions and would advance to compete in different towns. I struggled with confidence and self-esteem in my high school years. It impacted me so much that when it was time to do our Driver's Education road tests, on my final drive, I ended up crashing the car into another incoming truck. That was how much I didn't believe in myself. Of course, one of my crazy cousins in that school told everyone and soon everyone knew I was the guy who "crashed the Driver's Ed car." I find it pretty funny to this day.

The best things about the change in schools was that I had mostly white friends in Cut Knife and now for the first time I could have both white and native friends; it was awesome. After school most days we would have volleyball practices and my coach made us work; even during school he would always have words of encouragement for me if he saw me in the hallways. He was a great role model. After my grade 10 high school season was complete, there was an outside of school volleyball club that was optional for athletes – but you had to pay to join. There was an under 16 team in North Battleford that was created, and the coach Andy Churko (former national volleyball champion), really wanted me to play. However, I couldn't afford the fee to play on the team. He found a way to make it happen for me by getting funding from a local charity; I will never forget his kindness. The club team helped me develop my skills as a player. That summer I continued to train myself at home; I purchased a volleyball set from Walmart to put up outside in my yard and that was where I trained to become a better player every day.

By grade 11, my coach and teammates were shocked to see how much I had improved as a player. As a result, I made the starting lineup. Andrew Albers was our star player – he was the most intense and fearless athlete I had ever played with. I remember him going up to every player, shaking them and screaming in their face, "Are you in this!" until the other person would scream "Yes!" He was the hardest worker on and off the court and excelled in multiple sports. Andrew would eventually become a Major League Pitcher for the Minnesota Twins and the Toronto BlueJays. I continued to commit myself to volleyball; my sister Kendra was just as passionate about the sport, as she was already a starter for her high school's women's team.

Throughout my high school years, my mom would spend most days at my Kokum's house watching over her; my Kokum needed help and my mom felt it was her responsibility to help as much as she could. I continued to visit my Kokum and often times she would speak only in Plains Cree to me about life and our culture. She continued to make me soup and bannock and would always ask me to eat when I would visit her house. In my spare time, I would continue to kick a ball around or play volleyball outside her house and she would watch out the window while sitting in her wheel chair. I was very close to my Kokum. Throughout the summer months, we would make small volleyball tournaments outside her house and all of our relatives would have a great time; she would come outside and watch all of us having fun. Those are the times I will always cherish, when all the family was around having a great time with our Kokum.

In grade 12, I found myself the captain of the John Paul II Crusaders Men's Volleyball Team. Throughout the season, my coach would often challenge me to think beyond high school and consider possibly becoming a teacher one day. Before that, I honestly thought I was going to become a carpenter – because I loved Industrial Arts class and making things out of nothing. I never thought of myself as "university material," but I took his advice and applied to become a teacher at the University of Saskatchewan.

After our final season of high school volleyball, we found ourselves without a club volleyball team to compete on because our club coach had moved away. There was a team we always competed with who had all First Nations athletes on it and they were all great players. My "white teammate" Adam and I decided to go and try out for the team. For the first time we found ourselves in an interesting situation where a "white person" was trying to be part of a First Nations team. Adam was an amazing player with a great sense of humor and we both were accepted with open arms. We were called "The Titans" and would eventually become the first predominantly First Nations Club Volleyball Team in Saskatchewan to win a Bronze Medal at provincials. Our coach was Simon Bird, who dedicated his time to helping a group of young First Nations men grow as athletes. Half of the starting lineup went on to play college volleyball after high school was over – something amazing and unheard of at the time. Simon was also the first First Nations coach to win Coach of the year from the Saskatchewan Volleyball Association.

After club season was done I played badminton – another sport I loved – and each year me and my doubles partner Brad Eishen would improve, until one season we made it all the way to provincials. Unfortunately, our prom was the night before the competition, which was being held 4 hours away. We got there around 3 a.m. and had a few hours sleep before our first match. We showed up still in our tuxedos and didn't make it to the finals.

I still don't know how my mom managed to pick me up from practices 4 to 5 times a week, with all the car troubles we had growing up. There was always one thing after the other, but she wanted us to participate in after school sports and so she found a way to make it happen for us.

As a graduating gift, my father gave me a 1998 Green Dodge Neon. I remember going to pick it up from his house on the rez and being excited to drive it home. However, I had to get my cousin Ashley to help me drive it home because it was a 5-speed car and I didn't at the time know how to drive it; she eventually taught me how and I was grateful to finally have my own car.

Not long after, I received a letter in the mail from the University of Saskatchewan. I was ready to open my acceptance letter. I was so excited and quickly opened the letter and it read: "Sorry to inform you that you have not been accepted." I was crushed and felt rejected. I knew that my grades weren't good but I had hoped I would get in anyway.

When you have a goal, and you believe in it strongly, you don't give up easily; I knew I wanted to do something other than live below the potential my role models saw in me. A blessing came shortly after that when a coach named Trent Mason called me to tell me that he was going to become a coach for Keyano College in Fort McMurray, Alberta, and would be delighted if I would play for them on a scholarship.

He also noted that I would only need a 60% average to get in to the college (I definitely had that!) – and so I applied and got in.

When I graduated high school, I didn't celebrate like most people do; I ended up hanging out with my mom and a few relatives, getting some food and then going home and starting to think of my future in college. That summer I took a job on the rez and cut grass all summer with several of my cousins; as crappy as the work was, it was fun to be able to spend time with them while working for $6.50 an hour. Our club coach Simon also brought a volleyball team to Arizona to compete in a North American Indigenous tournament that both my sister and I played in. It was the first time we travelled outside of the country and it was an amazing experience. The rest of the summer I was getting myself ready to leave the rez for the first time, but most importantly, to leave my mom, my Kokum and sisters for the first time. Volleyball had presented me with an opportunity to take my gift to another level and to obtain a college education.

IN ORDER TO GROW, YOU MUST BECOME UNCOMFORTABLE

College and Volleyball

AT THE END of the summer of 2005, I loaded up my car full of my belongings, said goodbye for the time being to my mom, sister and Kokum (I tried to hold back the tears, it was very hard) and headed off to Fort McMurray, Alberta, where most people would go to work in the oil fields but I was going to attend college and to play some volleyball. My mom sent me there with a list. It told me how to make food for myself, how to study effectively in school (she had taken university classes when I was in high school and earned very high grades), included a prayer in Cree and basically everything she could think of to help me transition effectively. It was the first time I had to look after myself and I was not prepared as well as I should have been.

When I arrived on campus, I was shown my new dorm room that I would be sharing with 5 other people. The roommate I would be living closest to was actually from Ile-a-la-Crosse, SK, a northern Metis community. His name was Brian and we both figured out that we were there to play on the men's volleyball team and we got along great. When we showed up to our first practice, there were actually 4 of us Indigenous players that had made the trip to play volleyball for Keyano College; it was awesome. We all found ourselves in the same boat that included getting lonesome for family and having a hard time feeding ourselves and basically adjusting to the college environment and area. After the first few months, Brian and I found ourselves to be the last Indigenous athletes who were still on the volleyball team and committed to our studies. Unfortunately, our two other First Nations brothers dropped out and went back home to their First Nations reservations.

Throughout college, I was in a relationship with a girl from back home. We had a hard time figuring out how our relationship was going to work with me being so far away; the distance would eventually sour things between us. I started to drink and party with the volleyball team and my college friends weekly; the college was surrounded by bars and even a strip club so there was easy access. I was living in Alberta; I was the legal drinking age of 18 years old; and I was going out very regularly, because that's what everyone else was doing. I witnessed many negative events in Fort McMurray while partying and saw people engage in drugs and other hardcore stuff; thankfully I knew to avoid the drug scene.

During practice we had an assistant coach that was always on my case and always pushing me harder than the other players. I always wondered why this guy hated me (at least I thought he did). One day at practice he stopped the drill and said, "what the hell is wrong with you!" and shoved me several feet back. Our other coaches and my teammates were in disbelief and after an awkward pause, we went back to our drills. Deep down I was angry and that practice I hit harder than I ever had before. To my surprise, he acknowledged that to the team at the end of practice. The assistant coach always seemed like he was holding anger within himself and he would take it out on the rest of us by screaming at us or throwing volleyballs as hard as he could at us. Another time he made me stand a few feet from the net and he began spiking volleyballs as hard as he could at me until he felt I had had enough. He had a weird coaching style, but I later realized that as negative and as humiliating as it was, it somehow made me a better player. At our first tournament in Red Deer, AB, during our second match, he called a timeout and pulled me aside and shouted at me in front of everyone, "What the f**k are you doing out there!" I was stunned as always, hung my head and let the anger swell up in me. The rest of the tournament I gave it everything I had and my coaches started to notice my potential. Our assistant coach would eventually get fired for other behavior and as bad of an experience as it was to have him give me a hard time, I am thankful for that because he toughened me up.

One challenge I dealt with as a volleyball player was my height. Although I was tall in the real world, I was short for volleyball; I was a very short middle position player at 6' 2" – most other middles on other college teams were 6' 5" and over – so I had to jump twice as hard to keep up with them. All the jumping started to impact my knees and I found myself icing and popping Advil before and after every game and practice. Yet, the hard work and resilience paid off: at the end of my first college season I was awarded Rookie of the Year. Despite all the challenges, I had made it through my first year of college. Thankfully, I also managed to pass all of my classes – except for one, psychology. However, that would be the last time I would fail a post-secondary class. Among other highlights that first year, during the season I was asked to be in a commercial for the college, marking my first time speaking on camera. You can actually watch it on YouTube and see how timid and shy my demeanor was back then.

After our first semester, my roommate Brian dropped out also and moved back to his home northern community, which left me the last Indigenous player on the team. To make matters worse, I found out that he committed suicide later that year. It was heartbreaking. He liked to talk about his family and community, and he wasn't afraid to stand up for himself. I remember shortly before he moved back home that he got in a fight with one of our teammates; the teammate taunted him and Brian really put a beating on him. He was always a good friend to me, an amazing volleyball player and was respectful to everyone around him. It was too bad to hear about his passing.

Throughout the year, I became great friends with a guy named Mozac Samson who was originally from Fiji. He played on our men's volleyball team and was built like a football player. We both shared many similarities between our cultures and we got along great and supported one another. Mozac would later get his Canadian citizenship and become a key player on the Team Canada Rugby Team. Mozac was a great friend who kept me feeling comfortable each time I would miss home or my family.

After my first year of college, I spent the summer in Sweetgrass First Nation. When I got home I realized that I actually lost weight from not eating enough and training too much. So that summer I started to lift weights and eat as much as I could and it started to pay off. It was also the summer that I went to the North American Indigenous Games to represent Saskatchewan in Denver, Colorado. We had an amazing team; most of our starting lineup had just finished their first year of college or university volleyball. We ended up having no problems with winning the tournament and claiming a gold medal – it was special. My sister Kendra was also at the games and won a silver medal; she was always one of the top players on her team. That summer I also took up a painting job in North Battleford with several of my cousins. It wasn't the most fun job but I was able to make a little money. The boss who hired me also didn't fulfill many of his promises, due to the amount of overtime I put in. That experience was the start of getting tired of working for other people and their agenda. The rest of the summer I spent training for the next season of volleyball, figuring out what I was going to do with the girl I was dating and spending time visiting my family and my Kokum. I used to like to bring her a bag of chips and we would enjoy each other's time and relax at her place, flipping between the two channels available on her TV.

When I made my way back to my 2nd year of college, unfortunately, so did the girl I was dating (worst decision I made that year). Having a girlfriend at college made it hard to focus on volleyball and my studies. We ended up having a hard time being faithful to one another and that would begin the downfall of our relationship. After the first semester, she ended up dropping out and moving back home. My sister Kendra was also at the same college, which was a great comfort. She was one of the best on her team and made the Alberta Colleges Athletic Conference All-Star team – she was that good. Kendra was also very gifted in soccer and probably could have made any college soccer team, if she had committed herself to it.

Throughout my final year at Keyano College I became the team captain, but my knees continued to give me problems and I wondered how much longer I could keep training everyday and still play games on the weekend with a day of rest on Sunday only to repeat it all over every week. Thankfully, we had the most talented volleyball player I would ever have as a teammate. His name was Alwyn Piche, a fluent Dene speaker who came from La Loche, SK. In high school, he would dominate and had a swing so hard that in every gymnasium we watched him play in, he would hit the ball so hard into the ground that it would bounce and slam the ceiling just as hard – it was incredible. Alwyn would inevitably be awarded the Most Valuable Player in the Canadian Colleges Athletic Association.

Alwyn and I would also become great friends, along with Chris Smith, who was also on our volleyball team and originally from Inuvik, Northwest Territories. All three of us were Indigenous athletes using our gifts to take us somewhere in life. One day, I got a call from my dad and he told me and my sister that he was in Fort McMurray for work and he wanted to take us for supper; we were happy to hear from him. We ended up having supper with him several times and he would buy us groceries and in a way it was him showing us that he was proud of us. I remember him showing up at my practice one day and in the middle of a drill, out of the corner of my eye, I saw him watching; that was a special moment for me.

On nights after games on our home court, the men's and women's team always went out for drinks and a bar to "celebrate" like many college athletes do. One night in particular turned out badly. We had just finished going to the bar and on our way back, my good friend on the women's team, Erin, and I decided to grab some pizza before walking back to the dorms to meet up with everyone. On our way walking out with our pizza we heard a women standing with a friend say, "Yeah, go home with your dirty Indian!" We both turned back towards her and in the blink of an eye I saw Erin charging after a lady that was double her size. They had a good battle and she put up a good fight with barely a scratch on her. After Erin was done with her, we started to walk back with our food and we could still hear her screaming derogatory words to me in the distance from the ground. I thanked Erin for what she did and told her that she didn't have to do that. She told me without hesitation, "I can't stand racist people, I will stand up for any of my friends." There would be other events that would happen throughout my time there; I just got better at ignoring them.

After 2 years at Keyano College, I applied again to the University of Saskatchewan, and this time got into the Arts & Science Program. However, they only accepted over half of the credits that I had earned in college (what a bummer!). Nonetheless I was happy to be accepted into university, where my next goal was to obtain a degree. When I left Fort McMurray, I moved back to the rez and got my first summer job that I was excited to have, SGI Salvage (Saskatchewan Government Insurance). I would spend the next three summers working there in between university semesters. That summer, I also bought my mom a car with the scholarship money I had received from my final year of playing college volleyball. I always tried to look after her.

Throughout the summer, I learned many new skills during my time at SGI Salvage. I was taught how to drive a forklift, ship vehicle parts, the anatomy of vehicles, etc. During this time, I was driving to work every morning in the 1998 Dodge Green Neon that my dad had gifted me in grade 12. One day during work, I was required to ship a car part on the bus across town. I headed out with the Chevrolet 1500 Crew Cab company truck and on my way back, I was making the final turn towards our workplace when suddenly I was rear-ended by a group of high school kids on lunch break. They hit the rear bumper so hard that I thought for sure there was major damage. I got out of the truck and went back to see if they were ok and thankfully they were. I looked at his small 4 door car and it was smashed up badly and was leaking antifreeze all over the road. I then looked back at the truck bumper and only saw a small dent the size of a quarter and couldn't believe it. When I got back to work, the staff thought it was pretty funny; I was lucky I didn't get bad whiplash that day and proceeded to carry on with my day.

A week later at the same final turn to work, I was coming back from lunch break and driving my car when suddenly another car blew through a "stop sign" and crushed the passenger side of my car; the air bags blew up, they knocked the wind out of me and the impact knocked us into the opposite lane (luckily the other side slammed on their brakes, otherwise I would have been hit twice). A nearby person pulled me out of the vehicle and checked me over to see if I was ok (thankfully I was). I was cut on my face – because my clipboard hit the airbag and then smacked my face. Somehow my "Whopper" from Burger King made it out ok. After the ambulance and police arrived, they drove me back to work and my boss sent me home due to whiplash; a few days later a co-worker nicknamed me "crash." With the money I got for my insurance, I was able to buy a 2002 Pontiac Sunfire that would last me throughout university.

That summer I was closer to home and would continually make more time to visit elders back home, such as my Kokum Emma and my mom's brother Ernie. I sought help from them many times on issues related to our culture and life teachings. There were countless times when their knowledge has helped me along my journey. My Kokum Emma liked to have a treat once in a while and I would enjoy bringing her a wagon wheel or a bag of chips just like she used to do for me as kid. I always knew she was proud of me for attending university.

It would also be my first time participating in a cultural ceremony, one that was held during the summer months. This would be instrumental in enabling me to make better choices with my lifestyle in the future. My uncle Ernie made time for me when I had questions about my future and our culture and gave me guidance. Ernie along with his older brother Benny were prominent elders back home and were highly respected everywhere they went. They always encouraged everyone to have faith in the Creator and attend our Traditional Cultural events.

As the summer of 2007 was coming to a close, I was getting ready for life away from the rez once again and for moving to Saskatoon. That summer, I applied and received my first credit card and used it to buy some new volleyball equipment online (little did I know I was building my credit by using and paying off this credit card). After a few purchases, I noticed an email in my inbox that was promoting the Education Program being offered in North Battleford. On the poster, it had a contact number and as nervous as I was, I picked up the phone during my lunch break and began dialing the number. This is the power of the cold call. On the other end of the line was the director of the program, Orest Murawsky, and he greeted me pleasantly.

"Hello," he said. "This is the Indian Teacher Education Program, Orest Murawsky speaking."

"Hello Orest," I said. "My name is Kendal Netmaker and I applied to your program when I graduated in 2005 and I never got in, what do I have to do to get into your program?"

After just 5 minutes on the phone with Murawsky discussing my work ethic and my goals, I was accepted into the program I had been denied access to after graduating high school. Sometimes things work out for people who are driven to change and are willing to do what most people are afraid to do. I would also find out that in order to get fully accepted into the College of Education at the University of Saskatchewan, I would need to have a grade point average of 70% or more in five core subjects. At the time, I had a grade point average of under 70% in four out of five subjects. But I managed to get into the University anyway because the average for the fifth subject, Christian Ethics (mandatory class back then), was nearly 90%, pulling up my overall average to 70%. The remainder of the summer was spent with my Kokum, my mom, and sisters, until the big move to Saskatoon.

SOMETIMES YOU NEED TO LEARN THE HARD WAY

University, Survival, Hard Lessons

THE FIRST PLACE I lived was a rented room in a townhouse shared with a younger couple. Everything was fine for the first week, and then things started to become awkward. My food would go missing, they started asking for rides to pick up weed at their drug dealer's house and I started to feel very uncomfortable. But what really got my upset was when they started getting high in the house. That is one thing I don't put up with, so I moved out and was forced to pay a premium price to live by myself in a small one-bedroom basement suite that cost me $650 per month. My car and gas expenses were $150/month; I had a "pay as you go" flip phone that cost around $50 per month; all of which left me with around $100 per month for food and any other costs that would come up. That $100 a month would have never been enough to live on. But thanks to volleyball, I was able to support myself; my friends and I formed the Moose Meat Volleyball Team and became one of the top men's teams in the province. We attended tournaments every weekend and placed in the top 3 at most of them. This meant I was bringing home a few hundred dollars each weekend. That was literally how I survived on my own; I wouldn't have been able to do it without the sport of volleyball.

My sister was also attending the same university as me, en route to becoming a teacher one day. Kendra would also try out and make the University of Saskatchewan Women's Volleyball team. Unfortunately a month into her training, she broke her foot, which ended her career that year. She would eventually come back and continue playing in elite tournaments and excel in volleyball and soccer while obtaining her degree.

Adjusting to another year of school and living alone had many challenges. One of the challenges was staying focused on my studies and where I wanted to head in my life. Partying and girls would force me off track many times in my first year of university. For many years I had been a shy, quiet kid with low self-esteem and when I finally found my confidence, I combined it with partying and alcohol. It was a devastating combo that would get me into trouble. I found myself in and out of various relationships and womanizing would eventually get the best of me. I was a young man who didn't care to be in a relationship for the long-term. I was very selfish and I only cared to have a girl around me to "feel like I was a man" or "numb my loneliness." It was stupid. This type of immature thinking would catch up with me later on.

At the end of my first year of University in 2008, I moved back to the rez and resumed my summer job at SGI salvage until the fall. I found myself attracting more and more problems into my life because I was regularly partying with friends and not staying focused on the teachings my mom and elders would pass on to me. When I would go out partying, I would be too ashamed to come back to my mom's house drunk, so I would stay away until I sobered up.

That summer I decided it was a "cool" idea to have several girlfriends at the same time (I was an idiot for thinking this would work). That didn't last long after one particularly wild night out in Saskatoon. I was with one of the girls. We pulled up to the club, got out of the car and before we could go inside, a group of 8 to 10 guys began running over to me. I immediately ran back to the car, jumped in and turned the ignition on, while they were pounding the windshield and door windows. Somehow they weren't able to break the glass and I was able to spin out of there and to safety. This girl's ex boyfriend was very unhappy with my decision to see his ex girlfriend and found an opportunity to try and lay a beating on me. It felt like someone was looking out for me that night. My head was so out of whack that I didn't care if the girls I were seeing just got out of long-term relationships. And it nearly resulted in me getting the crap kicked out of me. Even with that incident, it didn't smarten me up and I continued acting like a fool.

That summer in between all of that I went to work, continued to visit my Kokum and elders who taught me many things. I remember one of my uncles gave my mom some encouraging words to keep moving forward because he sensed I was going in the wrong direction in my life. Many elders have gifts and senses and he knew I was capable of more than the life I was trying to live. I was trying to live that life that I had grown up around where my cousins and family members would drink and party and attract many problems for themselves because of that negative lifestyle. I was conditioned by my environment and I needed to change that to give myself a chance at what my mom was told. As an infant my mother was told by an East Indian Doctor that "This one is going to be a smart boy." She asked him how he knew but he didn't reply; she told me this when she saw me heading in a negative direction.

I participated in a cultural ceremony again that summer; it made me feel so good that I began to think of one day quitting drinking and going after the goals I wanted to achieve with my life. During the summer of 2008, I was asked to attend a Leadership Summit in Toronto. There were two problems I faced: I was 20 years old and had never owned a suit; and I had never been on an airplane in my life. Thankfully I had some savings from the summer job and I went back to the "Sears Catalog" and began to order myself a suit (thankfully it fit ok). I flew to Toronto and the conference opened up my eyes to the business world and I was very intrigued by the opportunity. I remembered how I used to picture myself as a kid living on the rez – of me one day wearing a business suit. During that conference, I was asked to sit on a panel with two other men in which we would discuss how working for the government as a student was benefiting us and our future. I was terrified, but I also used the panel as an opportunity to tell a bit of my story, which made it easier for me to talk in front of people.

In the fall of 2008, I moved in with my one of my friends into a two-bedroom apartment and was ready to tackle another year of university. The year started out like any other when suddenly I started to receive phone calls about family members who were dying. It seemed like back to back people were passing away and it was awful and I had a hard time focusing on my studies. My Kokum Emma passed away on October 3rd, 2008, and I was devastated. I ended up having to drop out of half of my classes that semester; over the next few years, I would end up learning several of the hardest lessons of my 20s.

That fall I noticed a beautiful girl who I was attracted to in a way that I had never been with a stranger before. She was much shorter than I was and had a beautiful glow to her that I was not used to seeing. Her name was Rachel and she was a first-year university student studying to become a teacher. I remember seeing her around campus and out at events we both attended. Rachel and I eventually started seeing each other. I would take her out for coffee, play pool and when I found myself getting close to her, my immature thinking would get in the way and try to stop me. It made it difficult to commit myself to a girl that I was into because of bad relationships I put myself into in the past. I didn't want to believe that Rachel could be "the one" for me, although deep down I knew that I had found her.

One day not long after getting closer to Rachel, I received a call from a woman whom I had hooked up with a few months earlier; she told me that I might become a father next year. I was shocked. I didn't know how to tell Rachel or anyone else for that matter so I kept it to myself for several months. The other woman continued to keep in contact with me and had me believing that we were having a child together before the baby was even born yet. The pressure was getting to me and I had a hard time focusing on school and continued to party to numb the pressure. This lifestyle eventually made me make one of the worst decisions any human being can make.

It was the coldest day of the year. It was December 2008 and the temperature was a record breaking -52 Degrees Celsius with the wind chill. My cousin was going to get married that day and she had asked me to be a groomsman, which I gladly accepted. It was so cold outside that we had to let our vehicles run during the whole wedding ceremony or they might not have started later on. After the wedding ceremony, the wedding party rented a limo and cruised to North Battleford to begin the celebration – which, of course, involved alcohol. We eventually made our way back to Moosomin First Nation, where the reception and dance was taking place. Things were going well, and we continued to have drinks, make toasts to the beautiful couple and so on. The whole night, I felt as though I barely drank because I felt pretty "normal." The wedding dance was winding down and I decided that I was going to crash at my cousin's place which was about 2 kilometers away from the dance. We grabbed some plates of food before we headed out to his place and then we jumped into my 1998 green Dodge Neon and were ready to head off to his place. For some reason, he decided he was going to stick around a little longer, so he gave me his house key and we agreed that I was going to drive to his place because it was "not even far" and "I felt fine." So off I went, alone, at about 2 a.m., driving in the freezing cold.

I took the first right turn and within 100 meters I suddenly found myself driving on down the right side of the road – nearly impossible to drive out of for any vehicle because it was so steep and packed with snow. I don't know what happened after that. I felt like I was in shock. I focused as best I could and just used whatever reactions I had left in me and made every effort to get this tiny car back on the road; if I were to get stuck there, no one would be able to see me that far down the ditch and I'd be trapped for hours. At that temperature, at that time of night, I would have likely frozen to death. Somehow I made it back on the road and back to my cousin's house, where I quickly sobered up. Again, I felt like someone was watching over me. That night I made a decision that I wouldn't do anything like that again. I was ashamed of myself.

In early 2009, I was forced to enroll in 6 classes to make

up for the previous semester. I finally gave in and told Rachel about the possibly of me becoming a father in the coming months. She was heartbroken. We broke up and I didn't want to put her through what was to come because she didn't deserve it. We found ourselves coming back together. Still deep down, I found it hard to fully commit myself to her because I was now being controlled emotionally by the possible "mother of my future child." She put me through many situations that always messed with my emotional state from "If the child is yours, this will happen" and so forth. After my last semester before heading back home to the rez to work for the summer at SGI salvage, I knew sooner or later I would have to tell my mother of the situation I was facing.

It would be my last summer working at the salvage and I was looking forward to what would happen next. In my downtime, I would make things like a weight set out of rocks and old plastic containers or a balance board out of scrap wood and pipes. Coffee breaks would be the one thing I didn't look forward to. Some of the staff took it upon themselves to use it as a "complain about how bad life is" time every day. After being around that each day, it starts to affect the way that you think. You become part of who you are around and I found myself thinking more negatively. I would eventually have to take coffee breaks out of the meeting room and spend time alone.

One day in July that summer during work I received a phone call from the "other woman" and she told me that she had a boy that day and he had all of my features and looked

"Native." She refused to get a blood test to confirm paternity, so I did what I thought was the right thing and stepped in and became the father. Apparently the other guy she had been dating was a white guy with blonde hair. I knew that I had to tell my mom, so that evening after work I told my mom that, "I think I might be a dad" and explained the situation. My mom was shocked as anyone would be, and we both drove to Prince Albert, SK that evening to meet my son. When we walked into the hospital room, I immediately took the boy as my own and I knew I had to step up to become a father for him. My mom was now a grandmother or Kokum to the boy and she was happy as any grandparent would be. I continued to go see my boy when I had time off of work, send money for diapers, formula and just did what I could to be a father and be there for my son. Things were ok for the first few months; the other women would also visit a few times closer to home so that our son could be seen by more family members. I grew very close with him and loved him. Rachel continued to be by my side during all of this.

One day the other women and I were talking and she began to talk about her past and she eventually opened up about "selling drugs" and even doing this during her pregnancy. This was something I was not ready for. If she was doing that while pregnant, there was good chance that she was still doing it, and the clues began to appear with each visit I would make to visit our son in Prince Albert. She became more moody and demanded more from me. We would make plans so I could come and see our son and after I was already halfway there, she would tell me that I couldn't see him. She began to use our son as a way to get what she wanted, whether it was money, or control of another person. Rachel saw it in my behavior; I was always worried about my son and what was going on.

That fall I went back to the University of Saskatchewan to complete my remaining two semesters before my teaching internship. During the year I knew I had to find a way to get custody of my son after everything the woman had told me about her past and present. She refused to let me raise our son no matter how many times I asked. My mom was ready to step in and give me a hand if that ever happened. By early 2010 and into my second semester, Rachel and I decided to rent a small one-bedroom apartment and officially move in with each other.

The weeks leading up to this day I had been working on my first business plan for Moose Meat Apparel. It was a clothing brand that was named after the volleyball team my friends and I had founded. I wanted to create a clothing brand that would help fund other Youth Moose Meat Volleyball teams in the future. All of my teammates had funny nicknames like: Moose Knuckle, Moose Lips, Moose Legz, Moose Ears, etc. and we were very popular and I knew selling shirts would be a hit. One day I finished class and I was headed back to the apartment Rachel and I lived in. I jumped on the bus and decided to get off at the nearest "Staples" store and look at the business planning software, to make my plan look sharp. I only had $100 left on my credit card and that's what the "Business Plan Pro" software cost. I took a chance and bought it and went back to wait for the bus to head home and try not to tell Rachel about it, as I knew she would be worried about the money. As I got on the next Saskatoon city bus, who do I see? My beautiful Rachel watching me walk on to the bus with a "Staples" bag in hand. It was hard but I had to explain to her why I maxed out my credit card. It was obviously not an easy conversation to have, but she always supported me.

I decided to get legal advice and since I was a poor student, I had to consult with a "legal aid" lawyer. Legal Aid is a free service to anyone who is living below the normal standard of living. I went to a few sessions and explained my case and the big obstacle was determining a paternity test, which I agreed to do. When the other woman found out about me finding a lawyer and doing the paternity test, she was very unhappy about it and began to isolate me from our son. She refused to take our son in to do the paternity test. As time went on, I rarely saw him. One day out of nowhere, she called me in May 2010 and said that I can come and pick him up for a few weeks because she needed "a break." I immediately drove to Prince Albert, picked up my son and drove him to my mom's house in Sweetgrass First Nation.

When I arrived at the rez with my son, my mom was happy and she began to help me with the days ahead as I was finishing up my business plan and my final exams for that semester. I told the other woman that I was going to keep our son from now on because I feared for his safety and I also believed she was still selling drugs. She was furious about that decision and I watched over him for the next few weeks. One day I drove back to Saskatoon and prepared to compete in my first business plan competition the next day where I had to give a 5 minute "pitch" of my idea and how it needed start up money to continue. I made a mistake by posting on Facebook where I was (in Saskatoon). The other woman saw that post and immediately drove several hours to my mom's house on the rez; when my mom opened the door she pushed past my mom and abducted her own child. My mom was heartbroken when she told me the news. I was so upset; I wanted to quit the competition I was in and just go back home to be with my mom. There was nothing the police could do and that would be the last time I would see my son.

The next day at the competition I felt lifeless; I felt like not myself. I showed up anyway, did my pitch (I honestly thought I did horrible). That evening at the gala, Rachel showed up with me and was there to support me as always. That night I won first place and $6000 to launch Moose Meat Apparel. I was shocked and it took me completely by surprise. I started to buy t-shirts and hoodies and put a few Moose Meat designs on the shirts and began selling them on campus. That summer I also attended spring and summer classes; so I started selling the apparel to my classmates and professors out of my backpack and created an online store.

In June 2010, I received a call from my lawyer. I was just getting out of class when the phone rang. She sounded happy when she asked to speak to me for a few minutes. She said, "Kendal, we sent the letter for our first court date for custody of the boy and within days of her receiving that notice, she decided to do the paternity test. I have some news. You are not the father of this boy." After a minute of silence, I hung up. I was devastated. Just like that, he was no longer my son. Someone whom I had loved and cared for was no longer mine. I called my mom and she began to cry and weep. It was the hardest thing I had to tell her. The past 20 months, I had been made to believe that I was a father; I was manipulated, emotionally abused and through it all, Rachel was always there for me. I don't blame the other woman for what happened; my past selfish decisions were the reason for being in that situation. I decided from that moment that I was going to turn my pain into fuel. Turn my pain into my gain for future success. The following month in July 2010, Rachel and I found out we were going to have a child together.

That coming fall, I had to move back to my rez because I was completing my final teaching internship at Sakewew High School in North Battleford, SK. It was difficult to move and leave Rachel for four months in Saskatoon as she continued attending university that semester. That semester I was teaching First Nations youth from grades 10 to 12 various subjects. Most of these kids came from broken homes and I tried to be uplifting when they had time with me in my class because I could sense the pain most of them faced during their after school lives. During my internship, I also got invited to compete in a national Aboriginal pitch competition where celebrity judges like Robert Herjavec would be in attendance. I attended and pitched Moose Meat Apparel but I didn't place and it would be a learning experience for future business opportunities to come.

During that year I had a dream about my Kokum. She was at her house and I just walked in to her kitchen where she spent most of her time. I was so delighted to see her and she opened up her arms to give me a big hug and I remember clinging to her in that dream and weeping because I missed her so much. Behind my Kokum was a person whom I had no respect for due to their past behavior. In my dream I felt anger and was wondering why this person was in my dream and ruining this moment for me. When I woke up, I was in tears and continued to cry. That morning as I was driving to school I was wondering what this dream meant. As I pulled up to a "Stop" sign I noticed the vehicle license plate in front of me. It wrote "4GIVE" and I knew right at that moment what that dream was about. In our Native culture, dreams can contain messages. My Kokum gave me a message to forgive my past and the people who have hurt me. I decided to work on myself to be a better partner to Rachel, a better son to my mom and a better person overall so I could help myself to keep moving forward.

By the end of 2010, I had completed my internship and was set to graduate with my Bachelor of Education that spring. I moved back to Saskatoon with my girlfriend Rachel to prepare for our child to be born in early 2011 and I also decided to enroll in one more semester to complete a second degree in Indigenous Studies.

In my final semester of University in March 2011, I realized that Moose Meat Apparel was not going to work. I couldn't trademark the name and protect it because it conflicted with similar names of companies that had rights to sell physical goods. During this time I was talking with my friend, Neal Mcleod, on Facebook about the situation and he said, "Why don't you just rename it Neechie Gear?" After doing my research, the word Neechie is a slang form of "friend" in the Plains Cree language (commonly used between men as "brother") which stems from the original word: Niwicewakan (my friend). Neal had provided a possible solution to the problem I was facing. I felt like a failure because I knew that I was going to have to start over after a year of progress. Right before making the decision to close down the brand, I was awarded Saskatchewan Student Entrepreneur of the Year and had been featured nationally in the Globe & Mail. So to come out and say that I was going to try and start over was a nightmare for me. I did it anyway and people thought I was an idiot for doing so. But I felt like I had no other choice.

I began constructing a new business plan and was set to enter several business planning competitions with my new brand name: Neechie Gear. I had a mission to empower youth through sports by donating a portion of profits towards helping kids who were once like me. I remember reaching out to several business people in Saskatoon and taking them out for coffee at Tim Horton's, because I couldn't afford Starbucks yet. I sat there with a notepad and pen and would take as many notes as I could to try and make the business idea work. After several weeks of learning how to write a business plan, I submitted it to numerous competitions. On April 3, 2011, my son Keanu was born and my life would change for the better. That night we spent in the hospital I would finish my business plan while I watched Rachel holding our sleeping, newborn son in her arms. In that moment, I knew things were going to change for the better for us. I did my final revision and pressed the "Send" button in hopes of making it into the final round of the competitions.

Several days later, Rachel finished her finals for that semester and we were adjusting to being new parents when I received phone calls telling me that I was a finalist for several competitions. I would now have to learn how to give the best "business pitch" I could deliver. For the days leading up to the final presentations, I was so nervous; I spent nights at the University of Saskatchewan in big empty classrooms practicing my presentation in front of no one. I had to imagine that there were thousands of people in attendance. It was very difficult, but it allowed me to prepare and gave me the confidence to show up and do the best job possible. The key was getting me to show up. When I did, my heart was racing, I felt sweat forming on my forehead and I had so much nervous adrenaline running through my body. In the back of the stages I would do stretches, pushups and jump around like I was getting ready for a volleyball match. Thankfully I placed in several of the competitions. I walked out with over $16k in prize money, which allowed me to order my first batch of t-shirts and Neechie Gear was born.

I had just finished two degrees from the University of Saskatchewan and was venturing off into a field where I had no clue how to begin. I started Neechie Gear out of my one-bedroom apartment, while Rachel was finishing her degree and our son was still an infant. I had no clue how I was going to make it happen, but I kept trying things everyday and found myself staying up until after midnight each night trying to figure out how to run and grow a business. My first store was that apartment. People would buzz #203 and would ask, "Hey! Is this Neechie Gear?" And people would buy from our storage closet, where I had put a few clothing racks and did my best to display the apparel. I had a wireless debit/credit card machine where people could pay for the items they bought. It was cool because it was working. I started to work on the online store and social media pages and I would push my products online.

While the company was getting going, I found myself taking a $13/hr. job just to make sure my family had food on the table. My mom would come to the city every week to watch our son while Rachel was in school and I was trying to make my business work. Both of our mothers would be a big help to us. Rachel's mom helped us by lending us a vehicle to use when Keanu was born (my car would break down and we couldn't afford to buy another one) and even bought us baby essentials (we were so unprepared). My mom would continue to spend days with us and watched Keanu just like my Kokum used to do for me at his age. Throughout all of this happening, we were living below our means, something which would eventually become an advantage to growing Neechie Gear.

GROWING A COMPANY
FROM NOTHING

Launching a Business

IN THE FALL of 2011 we found ourselves in line waiting to apply for social assistance in downtown Saskatoon. Through the whole process we were treated very poorly and felt much judged. They made us feel bad for being there. I hated the entire process and told myself that I didn't want to be in that situation again and it fuelled me to want to be successful in business so I could support my family. We ended up leaving that office with no assistance and unsure of how we were going to make it. Luckily I found a contract position with the Saskatoon Tribal Council that would help pay our bills for the remaining few months of 2011. During this time, I was invited to be part of the Canadian Delegation that would attend the Global Young Entrepreneur Summit in Nice, France, with 30 outstanding entrepreneurs that I felt I couldn't be compared to yet. It was an amazing event and my first time flying overseas. The experience of being around successful people made me crave that level of success. I also noticed my circle of friends becoming smaller as I focused my time on growing my business and spending time with Rachel and Keanu.

The hardest part was turning away incredible job opportunities that paid $50k to $60k per year because the companies wouldn't allow me to run my business on the side. Most people would probably think I was nuts to turn away those kinds of opportunities, when we were struggling so badly. But I knew that if I was going to make my business a success, I needed to dedicate 100% of my focus and energy towards it. At the end of 2011, I had a conversation with Rachel and told her: "I am going to go 100% into my business. I have no idea how I am going to feed us and pay rent, but I know that if I don't give this everything I have, it won't go anywhere. I need your support." Crazy enough, she supported me through it all. 2011 was the year I also decided to live a sober life so I could focus on becoming a better partner to Rachel and a better dad for Keanu.

My dad would stop in here and there throughout my life and one day he decided to stop in to see his grandson Keanu. It would end up being a long visit and one of the few times where I would have all of his attention. We talked and talked and he showed me he cared with his words. He gave wisdom and told me he was "proud of me." After he left our apartment, I went into our bedroom and wept. It was the first time my dad had ever shown that side of himself to me and it meant a lot; I had always wanted that as a child. Things like that happen for a reason and I do everything I can to be there for my children the way I wished my father had been there for me.

In early 2012, I rented an office in downtown Saskatoon, where I would take Neechie Gear out of my apartment and focus on growing the brand. People would ask me what I thought Neechie Gear would become or whether I thought it could take off one day. I told them that "I was going to create the next Lululemon" and they would often just laugh or act like they thought I was crazy. I learned quickly to keep my big goals to myself. I had to separate myself from all the negativity that was out there from friends, customers and even some family members. It was extremely hard on me. I was trying to grow a business and keep myself positive in believing that things were going to work out and I didn't need anyone telling me otherwise. I started working at that office and people started to treat it like a real retail store, showing up to buy hoodies and shirts from there. It was neat to see that people were coming to find me to buy my brand.

Because Rachel was an amazing student, she won several scholarships/bursaries that kept us afloat for 2 or 3 months and took the pressure off of me to support the family, enabling me to go all in on my business. We continued to work with what we had. We would take t-shirt photos on white paper we bought from the dollar store, using an old digital camera that Rachel owned. We would upload t-shirts photos to the site I designed (it was pretty bad). Our stock was in our storage room and my office was in our living room. One day I had an idea (one of my worst decisions) to buy a screen printing machine to "save money" on my costs, so we could have a higher profit margin on each t-shirt and hoodie we sold.

I had a fully operational factory happening in my one-bedroom apartment. I would get the screen ready in my storage room, take it to my bathtub to blast it with water, so the design would come through, load the screen on the screen printer, put ink on the screen, get the blank shirt ready, squeegee the ink onto the shirt, take the shirt off and heat it with a heater on my balcony until the ink was hard and was ready to be sold. Genius, right? Wrong! I lost thousands thinking I was going to save and make more money this way. What really happened was I made so many mistakes, wasted hours of my time learning about screen printing when what I should have been doing in the first place was focusing on selling my products. That was what I was good at. I was not good at playing "art class." I eventually sold my equipment to my friend Steve, who was the founder of Hardpressed, and he began to print our garments for us. He was amazing at it and I focused on selling and branding. The thing that separated us from every other brand was our story. I focused on telling our story as many times as I could and in as many ways as possible.

One day we got a big break. We got a call from a local mall in Saskatoon telling me that we had won a rent-free kiosk for 3 months and all I had to do was make sure there was staff there during mall hours to keep it running. I had put everything I had in the bank account into purchasing more apparel and designs to make sure we had enough to keep the cart running for several weeks (or so I thought). Within the first few weeks we launched we nearly sold out of our clothing and I kept my printer up late at night just to keep up with our clothing sales.

The next thing I had to figure out was finding a few staffers to run the kiosk while I was taking care of everything else. My first employee was a lady twice my age and people would tell her, "You must be so proud of your son." My first bookkeeper even tried to steal from me by forging a cheque in my name and thinking a 24-year old First Nations entrepreneur wasn't going to look at his bank statements. These would be among several growing pains we would face.

After the three months were over, the mall management was impressed with us making over $50k in sales during the timeline and they offered us a 500-square foot retail space steps away from the kiosk. It was a big decision as to whether to do it, because I would have to totally renovate it, order more stock, design it, etc. When you want to create something big, you have to go all in and that was the decision I made by signing a 3-year lease on that location.

So for the next two weeks I was in that store from 9 p.m. to 3 a.m. painting, putting retail equipment together, merchandising and making sure everything was working with our software. That summer, on July 1, 2012, we were the first 100% Indigenous owned clothing company in Canada to launch a branded store in a mainstream mall. A few months later we opened a pop-up store in another city called Prince Albert for 6 weeks leading up to Christmas. For the first time, in one month, our company produced over $100k in revenue and that was when I knew that we were onto something.

During this period, I was coaching Neechie Gear volleyball club teams that our company helped fund with profits from Neechie Gear; we would eventually partner with other charities and donate thousands of dollars to those who had similar missions to help kids through sports. We had athletes from all over Saskatchewan playing on our teams; it was amazing because we would eventually see some of our athletes go onto play college sports and attend post-secondary institutions after graduating. That year we were blessed to win awards and even met Prince Charles. We gifted him with a hand beaded Neechie Gear medallion. The craziest part was that my mom actually made a medallion in the 90s and her oldest brother Benny Weenie met with Prince Charles when he was in Saskatoon and gave him the medallion my mom made.

By the end of 2012, I proposed to my beautiful Rachel; she had been with me through the worst of times and was the key reason I wanted to improve my life. I knew that I would not be able to find someone like her again. After watching "Breaking Dawn" for the second time, I took Rachel down to the beautiful river view and proposed. She said "yes." Whew!

During the next few years Neechie Gear had three physical locations in different cities, an online store, nearly 30 retail outlets selling our brand across Canada and we were catering to corporations who wanted to buy custom apparel from us. It was a crazy time and I soon found myself dealing with many problems that most companies face when they are growing. First off, I managed all by myself and I didn't have a proper team in place to grow it effectively. I hired many retail staff (who are notoriously difficult to keep for the long term) and would continually have to cover shifts at different stores. Several times I thought we would go bankrupt and it stressed me out big time! I became a slave to my business; my health was bad due to not exercising; I was always eating fast food, drinking lots of coffee and spending way too much time away from my family. It was all catching up to me and I knew something had to change or I would end up in serious trouble. I knew that if I opened up 3 or 4 more stores in the other provinces where I had originally wanted to expand, I could become a millionaire within a few years. Where I came from, it was unheard of for a First Nations Entrepreneur to have made 7 figure sales in his mid-twenties. However, I chose not to pursue that road because I knew I wouldn't have been happy with the result. I was like a hamster in a wheel pushing very hard but going nowhere and my health, family and sanity was more important than that.

I was beginning to get asked to speak to First Nations communities, high schools and university classes about entrepreneurship, but mostly about my story, which I never thought anyone would care about. As I continued to share my story, I noticed the effect that it had on some people; seeing that talking about my experience was helpful and encouraging to others made me enjoy doing it. I won't forget the first presentation I got asked to do. It was in a northern Saskatchewan community in a high school. I got asked to give a short 3- to 5-minute speech. When they called my name, I jogged up to the stage in a nervous strut and ended up tripping on the stairs going up the stage. Of course everyone laughed, while my face was turning red and I felt blood trickle down my leg from the fall. I was holding a piece of paper with notes I had written down about what I wanted to say. All you could hear was the paper shaking through the microphone and I don't even remember exactly what I said to the audience. That was my first presentation and it was traumatizing. However, I kept showing up each time someone asked me to speak and I got used to and accepted my nerves and used them to make me a more interesting speaker.

One day I received an email about a business plan/pitch competition that was taking place in Phoenix, Arizona, hosted by the National Centre for American Indian Enterprise Development. I thought, like most people would, "This is too good to be true. I have no chance at ever winning that. Why even bother?" After rereading the email repeatedly, I finally ignored the negative voice in the back of my head (everyone has one) and applied to attend. I had to write a 50+ page business plan within a few days, fly myself (out of my own pocket) to Phoenix and show up to give a 30-second elevator pitch. If I made a mistake, I would be sent home. It was very intimidating, but I was confident that we had what it took to make the final round. When I arrived in Phoenix, I realized that out of 25 registrants, I was the only one from Canada who had taken a risk and showed up. The first round of pitching was very intimidating, as each person would get called up to a private room with a panel of champion judges from across the United States. The judges looked over my business plan and gave me

30 seconds to pitch and I thankfully made it to the final 5 where I was given 5 minutes to pitch. After that round I made it to the final 3 and pitched the next day at the finale. For the last pitch, we had 15 minutes and I used it to tell my story. I strongly believe because I included my story in the pitch and had a strong business model, we won $20,000 that day. I also believe we won because a few days before the competition we donated $1500 to KidSport, a national charity helping under-privileged youth play sports. When you give something, you get blessed with something in the future.

On February 12, 2014, Rachel and I had our girl Kaylie. I couldn't believe that we had two children and we were making our way through life together. They say that things change when you have a girl, and I would definitely agree with that statement. I felt even more driven to succeed from that day on. The day she was born I had a scheduled speaking engagement in northern Saskatchewan several hours away. Rachel knew that we needed the money and encouraged me to go even though I wanted to stay. A few hours after she had given birth, elated by the birth, but exhausted from the lack of sleep, I left to complete the speaking engagement. Having someone by your side supporting you is key to succeeding in life and business.

By 2014, much to my amazement, we were winning awards, and people were starting to take us seriously. I continued to get asked to speak in different communities spanning Canada. Futurpreneur would select me to represent Canada at the Global Entrepreneurship Congress in Moscow, Russia.

We were advised not to go at the time as Russia was trying to mess with Ukraine and military were everywhere; it was pretty scary but we still attended. Right after we touched back down in Canada, I got ready to meet another person whom I looked up to – a star from the hit show Shark Tank, Daymond John. I remember paying thousands of dollars in consulting fees and flying myself to New York City to meet with him at the FUBU headquarters located in the Empire State Building. I wanted to learn from the best and Daymond was one of the best in the industry. Not many people can say they have $6 billion in sales from a brand they created out of their house. The best takeaway I left with was that he was just like me, we were all human, but the person who was willing to get out there and produce results would inevitably be the one to succeed; I knew that I was up for that challenge. Mentorship would be a key role in my business life as I would continue to seek more guidance from others along the way.

In late 2014, an event occurred that changed my life for the better. I was touring with my good friend Dallas Soonias, who played for the Men's Team Canada Volleyball Team and professionally on the top teams around the world. We had always been good friends, as he had been a great ambassador for the Neechie Gear brand, and we decided to do a speaking tour together. We were speaking in Beardys & Okemasis First Nation on the last stretch of our tour. I had just finished speaking and in the corner of my eye I saw a non-Indigenous man approaching. He handed me a sticky note he had in his hand and said, "Kendal, great speech. I want you to YouTube this." And he turned and walked off. I had never seen him before in my life and I didn't even get a chance to catch his name. I thought little of the note he had given me, but I accepted it to be respectful. That night when I got home, I put the sticky note on my computer monitor and didn't think anything more about it; little did I know how much it would change my life.

A few months passed; it was Christmas break and I finally had some time to relax after a busy holiday shopping season at Neechie Gear. One night I was in my office while my son was playing beside me and I noticed the man's note still clinging to my monitor. It read: "Les Brown – You Deserve." I thought *why not* and searched on YouTube for Les Brown. I did not realize that I had just searched for one of the greatest motivational speakers of all time and that night I was hooked. I watched Brown for hours, bought his audio programs on my iPhone and listened to them when I was driving or when I was at home. I started finding other people – Zig Ziglar, Tony Robbins, and Jim Rohn – and I immersed myself in personal development, making it a priority to listen to the masters daily. Little by little, I began to notice change; I was becoming less negative and more optimistic; my family life was getting stronger; and I was exercising more. I wanted to find other ways of improving myself. This happened because I listened with an open mind and I thank that man for opening me up to a world I never knew existed.

MAKING THE DECISION!

On February 23, 2015, I finally identified and acknowledged my gift and made a decision to build upon it. I opened my audio recorder app on my iPhone and decided to record myself while my feelings were as strong as they ever were. I remember talking to myself and saying: "I have a vision for my future and it involves me becoming a speaker, creating a new company with my last name in the title, creating an academy and being a coach for people who are driven. But I have to make things easier for myself to do this. I have to let go of some things in my life in order to give it my all to become the best speaker and coach I can possibly become." I remember seeing a quote "In order to get something great, you have to give up something great" and I knew I had to start working on how I was going to do this to have everything I ever wanted for my family and me. I inevitably knew that I would have to give up my time in Neechie Gear if I were to ever become what I knew I could become in the speaking world.

During this time, Rachel and I would drive around the rich neighborhoods in Saskatoon and envision our lives having a big beautiful home like most of them. When I went for jogs, I would jog to those nice areas and create pictures of myself living in one of those homes. I started doing what other successful people were doing: I started buying books that taught me what I needed to learn; I invested in multiple online courses; I started building my network and reaching out to more and more mentors. I knew one day we could get that life, but I knew I had to start going after what was calling me, my gift – a speaking career. My mom would finally get a chance to hear me speak and I could see her in the audience shedding tears. I was conditioned unintentionally to keep striving for more from my mom. She was told by her mother not to tell her own children "How proud you are for them" but to instead tell them you are "happy for them" if they are doing well with their life. My mom would tell me she was "happy for me" and I always knew she was very proud of me. I didn't understand why other people's parents were always saying "how proud they were for their kids" and my mom wouldn't do that for me. I started to understand why – because it developed a hunger deep down in me to keep striving for more and not settle for anything less. There were very few people from my background at the time who had managed to leave the rez and become successful in the mainstream and I knew I had an opportunity to be a role model to many people.

That spring we were nominated out of hundreds around the world for the Youth Business International Entrepreneur of the Year Award. It was a shock when we received a call that we were shortlisted to the final 4 and we were to compete in the United Arab Emirates. What excited me most about the trip was being able to pitch in Dubai and bring my mentor Denis Prud'homme along. That whole trip he taught me so much about life and business and on top of that we were the runner-up for the award. For the first time in history an Indigenous entrepreneur was being celebrated on an international business stage. What a moment.

In the summer of 2015, I flew to Medellin, Colombia to go to an apparel trade show in hopes of finding some overseas suppliers. However, something changed when I got there. After the first day of the show I had a strong urge to really focus on becoming a speaker. The desire to help others was at an all-time high. I couldn't understand why it was happening when I was so far from home. For the remainder of the trip I started to map out how I was going to become one of the top Indigenous Speakers on the Globe. I started working backwards and seeing each step I would need to take to get there up until the day I was writing this all down. I began to study other successful speakers and see what they were doing. When you want to be successful you have to find other successful people and do what they do.

When I arrived home, I used all of my credit card points and booked myself a flight to Toronto, Ontario so I could attend an event called "Power of Success," where Les Brown, Tony Robbins, Bob Proctor, Dean Graziozi, Joe Polish, etc. were all speaking. Something deep down told me I had to be at this event. I watched how the speakers articulated their thoughts, how they used the stage and used their stories to wow the audience; it was beautiful. At the end of the event, I took a "Selfie" of myself on stage and I made a goal for myself that one day I was going to be speaking on stages like that in front of thousands of people.

On September 7, 2015 I married my beautiful wife Rachel Netmaker. She was the one person who had been able to see the good in me when I couldn't see it. She stayed with me when most people wouldn't have; she stayed with me through my darkest times and was always there to encourage me to keep moving forward. She deserves the best this world has to offer and I will continue to work my butt off to make sure she gets it.

I had made the decision to help others with my story and gifts. By the end of 2015, I started to work on how I could leverage what I knew and let people have access to the information through online training. I wanted people to be able to log in anywhere they had internet access and learn about entrepreneurship, success strategies, motivation, and other success stories and so on. By February 2016, I had made the decision to begin working on my next venture, the Netmaker Academy. It would be an academy built for Driven Entrepreneurs and Professionals. I started recording, editing and uploading video training to my site NetmakerAcademy. com. I wanted to help entrepreneurs and professionals achieve their goals faster through my academy and coaching program. I did countless free seminars and webinars for thousands of people who were interested in learning more about entrepreneurship, how to tell your story and personal development.

One day that spring I was driving back to Saskatoon after a business meeting when I received a strange phone call. The conversation was from an employee at Instagram who told me they had done some research on my background online and thought I would be an ideal candidate to meet the COO of Instagram and the Prime Minister in Ottawa in the near future. Of course I thought it was all fake. I mean, who calls someone out of the blue and gives them an offer like that? I waited for an email and soon enough it was confirmed and half dozen emerging leaders across Canada were selected to go to Ottawa for a VIP meeting with Instagram and Prime Minister Trudeau. Why did this all happen? I strongly believe your personal brand on social media and a Google search must be as clean as possible. People are no longer looking at a resume or application without going through Google and/or social media to see what you are all about. I got that opportunity because my search was positive enough for them to reach out. Start branding yourself online for opportunities that may come to you in the future.

Since making the decision to grow as a speaker, each year my engagements were keeping me on the go. In July 2016 I had a meeting with First Nations leader Wab Kinew, who was a best-selling First Nations author of "The Reason You Walk." I was lucky he made time to give me some advice on the book writing journey and what to prepare for. Nearly two years later I am finally able to share my story. Writing this has been one of the most difficult and healing experiences in my life thus far. I had to dig deep and revisit past pains. I hope you find inspiration in them to help you achieve your goals. The following chapters detail the 5 Steps to Succeed in Life and Business. They reflect lessons that I had to learn the hard way and lessons that other mentors have taught me. If you apply them to your life, I know you will see amazing results.

10 Success Principles

Think of your life as a skyscraper looking to reach the clouds. In order to reach the sky, you must build your foundation. If there are cracks in the foundation, you will eventually crumble. You may have seen famous celebrities who rise to fame and then suddenly fall down and have a hard time getting back up. It all relates back to their foundation. They have failed to repair the cracks and continue to move forward. You must be willing to work on your foundation as it is the main reason for you to continue to grow and move forward. It's hard to appreciate blessings if things are too easy. Hang in there. The best is yet to come.

If you follow these 10 Success Principles then you will be on the right track:

- You must be willing to believe in yourself more than others believe in you

- You must be willing to eliminate any distractions that will stop you from winning

- You must be willing to forgive your past and accept responsibility for your actions

- You must be willing to listen more than you speak

- You must be willing to build honest relationships and treat others with kindness

- You must be willing to take risks and become uncomfortable more often

- You must be willing to act and think like a success

- You must be willing to express sincere gratitude for everything you have been blessed with

- You must be willing to persist when everything seems to not be working out.

- You must be willing to dream BIG even though others may think you are crazy

Before we get into the next five steps I want to make it very clear that in order for them to work, you must be willing to work. You must be willing to put everything you have into them. You must be driven to succeed. If I have just described you, then let's get into the 5 Steps to Succeed in Business and Life! I want you to become who you were born to be and not what someone expects you to be. Desire is the mother of motivation. You must be DRIVEN!

STEP #1: MAKE A CHOICE, BECOME OBSESSED AND STAY INSPIRED!

Make a Choice!

THE GREATS IN the world that you see all over social media headlines all have one thing in common. Athletes like Kobe Bryant, entrepreneurs like Elon Musk, seminar leaders like Tony Robbins all have made a decision to be great at one thing. They all have made choices to maximize their gift. People who decide what they want in life know their strengths and weaknesses. They acknowledge and utilize their gift and focus on mastering it to its full potential. This means that you MUST make a decision of what you want to focus on. If you do not make this decision, you will become like other average people I have watched who have wasted their talents and abilities only to settle for a 9-to-5 job they hate going to that makes them sick over time. Or like the many athletes I have seen who have decided to turn to drugs and alcohol and waste their talents away. Or like the entrepreneurs I have seen that could have been millionaires only to continually compare themselves to other people and not follow their own paths and not realize the potential they already have within themselves. Or like the many dreamers I have coached who try to do too many things at once and don't focus on one thing they can master that aligns with their gifts. I could go on and on, but I hope you understand that you must make this decision today. Life is too precious to waste it doing something that is making you unhappy. People who make this choice will ultimately know what they want in their life and do what is necessary to obtain it. There will be times when you will have to do what you have to do until the day comes when you can do what you want to do. Inevitably you will find your path. Make a choice!

Become Obsessed!

Now I know what you may be thinking. Kendal, how do I know what choice to make in my life? I have no idea what that even feels like! Here is the best way I can explain this for you. Most people understand they have a unique gift that has allowed them to get to where they are up until this very moment. If no one has ever told you this, then let me be the first to: "You have talents and abilities that have been given to you for a reason. You are blessed and highly favored to succeed in your life. You have the potential to attract anything you want in your life. You have greatness within you. Now it is your turn to decide what you want and develop your greatness."

Have you ever noticed yourself continually thinking of something you have always wanted to do that keeps coming back into your mind? For some people it may be a project idea, some people have dreams of themselves pursuing a passion or maybe you continually get complimented on something you are good at doing that you could see yourself pursuing in the future? Everyone is different and for myself I knew I had to make that decision because I would stay up until 2 or 3 a.m. some nights just visualizing myself speaking and helping thousands of people. The dream always came back. The more I did what I was good at (helping others), the happier I was. It became an obsession and that is why you must decide what you want for your life. When you obsess over what you want, you attract more of the things that you desire in your mind through your work ethic. You start to attract the right people who will help you on your quest to obtain what it is you desire. When you are obsessed, the hard work doesn't feel like work, it feels like a necessary task to get to where you desire to be in your life. Become Obsessed!

Stay Inspired!

When your decision becomes an obsession, there will be many things that will suddenly go right in your life and business. It will actually make you feel like "this is too good to be true" because for once in your life, the stars have seemed to align for you and things are going right. The reality is that everyone will hit a wall. The wall is often described as an obstacle, major problem, etc. Now most people look at obstacles or problems as major hurdles and the weak often throw in the towel before even trying to look for a solution. Here is the reality: problems and obstacles are hidden opportunities put in your path so you can grow. Without pain and suffering it is hard to appreciate what is to come in your future. So try to look at these obstacles as opportunities to grow and try to think "what is this trying to teach me?" as opposed to the victim mentality where people feel like "Why me?" or "No matter what I do, trouble follows me" and so on. Those types of people rarely find happiness in their life and if they do, they are too negative to realize it is at their doorstep seeking their attention.

How do you stay positive when obstacles and problems arise? You must be careful what you put into your mind. Everything from who you associate with each day to what you listen to will impact you. I will go into this more in detail in the final step, but the message is – create a culture around your life where people are talking about possibilities as opposed to what is wrong in the world. If you hang with winners, you will become a winner. If you hang with losers, you will end up a loser. So in order to stay inspired through the hard times everyone faces, you must create an atmosphere around you that will support your dreams. Lastly, the more you struggled in your life from birth to the present, the bigger the opportunity waiting for you in the future – hang in there!

I want to share a quick story that illustrates what I mean by this. When I was in grade 10, I went to a new school to continue to have access to sports. During the first week of school, I didn't know many people and I often kept to myself as a shy young man with little self-confidence. One day we all got called down to the gymnasium to hear a motivational speaker who had come to speak to the school for the morning. As we all piled into the gymnasium, I went to the back of the room, as I often would, to try not to be noticed. The speaker got called up to the stage to present and for the next hour I was hooked on what the speaker was saying. I felt like the person was talking to me alone and I was so engaged that I was on the edge of my seat just watching. As the speaker closed the speech I told myself, *whatever it is that I decide to do with my life in the future, I am going to be doing something like that one day*. I had made a choice in grade 10 that I was going to be a speaker, even though I was the shyest kid in my class.

As I continued through high school, university and then several years into growing Neechie Gear, that dream would always come back to me. I would find myself up late at night visualizing myself as a speaker helping others to become all that they could be. In 2015, I made the decision that I was going to pursue it and it became an obsession as I practiced and practiced and did tours around Canada. I would occasionally hit walls where I would be forced to grow into a better speaker. I would run into negative people who thought I was too young to teach them these steps and would clearly turn off their minds when I would be their keynote speaker or confront me afterwards. As I was still running Neechie

Gear and trying to grow as a speaker at the same time, I was put through many obstacles such as: theft from customers, staff and even my first bookkeeper who attempted to forge a cheque in my name. So many things were stopping me from growing and I felt like a hamster in a wheel trying as hard as I could and not going very far. I started limiting my time with negative people who didn't value my future goals and I stayed inspired by finding people and mentors who helped me get closer and closer to my goals. I started to invest in myself and learn everything I could about helping other people as a speaker. I stopped trying to please other people and started to focus on what made me happy as an individual. I stopped caring what other people were thinking of me and once I started to practice these habits, I started to feel "free" and began to get further ahead much faster than I was able to before. I wanted to become who I was born to be and not what someone expected me to be. Make a choice, become obsessed and stay inspired!

9

STEP #2: PLAN, PREPARE AND EXPECT TO WIN!

Plan to Win

THIS PIECE IS inspired by the world's greatest motivator, Zig Ziglar. If you don't have a plan you are planning to fail. Every person I have looked up to has had to craft a plan of action for where they want to be in their life. I didn't realize this power until I started to do research on other successful people and found that their habits were a major contributing factor to their success journeys. There are many people (also myself) who stay "stuck" for years all because they have not made the decision and created a plan to achieve their ultimate goals.

There are 5 main reasons why people stay *stuck*:

1. Lack of direction
2. No plan to get toward their goals

3. They associate with the wrong people

4. They let their past and present circumstances determine their future

5. They don't know how to use what they already have

One of the things I noticed was that winners write their goals down often. Some do it daily or weekly. The key is to know your goals in the back of your mind so they stay there as you are performing your daily tasks. You want to always be thinking of them so you can attract opportunities and make the right decisions in your daily life that will take you closer to your goals. Now that you have made the decision about what you want to achieve, it's time to write it down. Start writing what it looks like. Describe the feeling once you reach your goals, write down all the details. Start by writing your lifetime goals from the decision you made in step #1. Keep it to three main goals and then write the required action you will need to do in order to reach those goals. Anything more than three is difficult to keep in your mind and will only create a greater struggle to remember. That is why you often see marketers use the magic number three in their marketing because they know the human mind can easily remember three main things at a time. I keep all my life goals to myself and I recommend you do the same. This is between you and the universe and so let's give it to the universe to help you attract your goals and reward you with your hard work.

Goal Card

Goal #1)_____.

Goal #2)_____.

Goal #3)_____.

x_____ Date:_____.

Required Action:

Goal #1)_____.

Required Action:_____

_____

_____.

Goal #2)_____.

Required Action:_____

_____

_____.

Goal #3)_____.

Required Action:_____

_____

_____.

Once you have written down your three goals, signed and dated them, you must keep this card with you at all times. Every morning take a moment to look at these goals; every evening take a moment; throughout your daily life you may find time to spare – so use it to look at these goals. You become what you think about most and this step is crucial to expecting to achieve your goals.

If you find you are not a writer, use your audio recorder like I did. I started to talk about what I wanted to do and all the necessary things I needed to in order to reach that goal. You should be able to write three lifetime goals and then break them down into yearly, monthly and daily goals. I recommend keeping your lifetime goal/yearly goals with you at all times. You can do this easily by buying a business card sized self-laminating card from a dollar store and creating a goal card. Plan to win!

Prepare to Win

There is no way to success without hard work. If anyone tells you otherwise, I would suggest removing them from your inner circle of friends. As Les Brown says: "You Gotta Be Hungry!" You must be willing to do the things you have to do in order to obtain the things you want to have.

Another thing that successful people do is put drawings or pictures in areas of their homes and workplaces that look like the goals they are trying to achieve in their lives. The more you see what you want and develop a picture in your mind, the easier it will be to attract opportunities that will get you closer to your goals. Some people call this a vision board. I personally didn't believe in the power of it when I first heard about it over 10 years ago. The past year I decided to give it a shot. I really tried to find images of the things I was trying to achieve; I put them up in my office and every morning I would look at them and think deeply about the feeling of having what was on the pictures on my wall. I really painted a picture in the back of my mind of what it would feel like to one day have everything on my wall. Then things started to freak me out. I had my goal card in my wallet all the time and throughout the day I would look at my goal card. In the morning I would look at my wall of the things I had wanted to work towards. I started attracting massive audiences to speak to (15,000 people) in several weeks. And within 6 months we had bought a house we never expected to be in until we were well into our late 30's. I began writing this book because I deeply wanted to help millions of people around the globe. So many things were starting to come together because I was working everyday towards the goals on my card and the images I had painted in the back of my mind. There are still things uncovering from these exercises I have given you. Keep updating your goals and keep growing and soon you will see beautiful things as a result of your hard work.

"Preparing to win" means: developing a work ethic that most people might find intimidating. There is no such thing as an overnight success. You must train your body and mind to be ready for the things to come in your life. I've personally spent hours upon hours working on my life and business without the world watching. The hardest part is working while your friends and family are enjoying themselves. You will need to sacrifice certain parts of life in order to obtain the abundance that most people wish they have.

Here is a quick story to illustrate the power of positive images and seeing them daily. My first day of university, I walked into the main entrance at the university of Saskatchewan and noticed there was a massive trade show selling posters to university students who would be walking through the hallways. I never had much money to spend on things and after a few days walking back and forth, I kept noticing a poster catching my eye. The poster was a man who had climbed a mountain – and I felt the urge to buy it. The poster cost me $20 and I hung it up on my wall for the remainder of my university days. Every day I would wake up to this poster and go to bed seeing this poster. The poster also had a quote on it that read: "He who is not courageous enough to take risks will accomplish nothing in life." When it came time to launch Neechie Gear several years later, I looked at that poster and thought of being courageous; I decided to take a leap of faith that things would one day work out if I put the effort in. And now you know the rest of the story. Words and images have power. Now it's up to you to use them to your advantage. Prepare to win!

Expect to Win

Have you ever noticed how some people continue to succeed in life and others lose consistently? The difference is goals – successful people have them. Winners have convinced themselves to win! People earn their goals by taking massive action everyday towards the goals they have painted in their mind.

Your self-image, the way you see yourself, determines your future. You must see yourself as already obtaining your goals. If you have followed these steps up until now, you have created the path that will allow you to reach your goal. The next trick is to be patient and have faith. You must have faith that it will come true. However you have been taught to have faith, pray often that way so that you will one day see your goal happen. Be grateful for all that has happened up until this point. You have earned the right to expect the best because you have planned and prepared for what is to come! Plan, prepare and expect to win!

STEP #3: TURNING YOUR PAIN INTO FUEL FOR SUCCESS

Turn Your Pain Into Gain!

WHATEVER YOU ARE going through, whatever you have gone through, you can change it. You can become anything you are willing to work for. A teaching that was passed from my Kokum to my mom was, "If you don't like how things are right now, change it when it's your time." I have heard stories from thousands of people who had to overcome insurmountable odds before achieving their goals. They have learned how to turn their pain into fuel for success. We all go through many obstacles in our lives. But what matters most is how you handle those obstacles. The best way to illustrate this for you is to share with you a story told by my sister Kendra. Here is her story:

"When I was a teenager, I used to blame other people

for my problems. I blamed my mom for my low self-esteem and I blamed my dad for my insecurity towards men. It was just easier to blame people that I cared about, rather than face my personal issues head on. As a teenager and young adult, I always had to have a boyfriend. I bounced from one relationship to the next in an attempt to avoid problems that I hadn't dealt with since childhood. Growing up, I didn't realize how much I needed my dad in my life. I wanted so badly to develop a positive father-daughter relationship with him, but there's only so much a daughter can do before losing hope. I remember wanting to call him all the time to give him updates on how well I was doing in school or how amazingly I played at my last soccer or volleyball game. Even more so, I wanted him to call me. There were so many times when I just wanted him to tell me that he was proud of me.

I became an angry teenager, and blamed everything wrong in my life on my parents. My mom was the easiest to blame, because she single parented me. I remember having so much resentment towards my mom that I was constantly doing the opposite of what she asked of me. As a teenager, I felt that she cared about me the least out of all my siblings and that she might be happier if I had just moved out of the house. When I matured some years later, I realized that this wasn't true, and that I should stop blaming her for all my problems. She was doing the best she could as a single parent with no support. I definitely gave her the hardest time out of all four of us siblings. She was pretty hard on me too, because I was the eldest daughter.

I had boyfriends from the age of 14, up until age 25. I think the longest break I had without one was around 6 months. Most of my relationships lasted a few months, if that. Having a boyfriend meant that I didn't have to be home half the time, especially during the summer months. It also gave me an excuse not to be around my family, who I felt were always giving me a hard time and didn't want me around. It also meant that I could receive the male affection that I longed for and didn't receive from my father while I was growing up. In the long run, I felt worse emotionally and mentally after every relationship. There were very few (less than a handful) boyfriends in my past that I can honestly say treated me with respect. A lot of times I dated a guy thinking that I could help him change. I always ignored my instincts and the red flags when entering into a new relationship. Don't get me wrong: there were a few good guys that I met along the way. For the most part, I learned some valuable life lessons.

Because I was incredibly stubborn and never listened to my mom, I had to learn things the hard way. When I say this, I'm specifically talking about relationships. My greatest life lesson came after giving birth to my sweet baby girl. It's amazing how one's whole perspective on life changes after becoming a parent. You become responsible for the life of another human being. After giving birth, my priorities completely changed. My baby girl saved me.

I met my daughter's dad when I was 24 years old. It was my university graduation night, and I was out at a bar with some friends to celebrate. From what I can recall (which isn't much because I was very intoxicated), I approached him that night and was very being very forward. We began dating shortly after and would see each other most days of the week. I thought he was the most amazing person I'd ever met, a total Prince Charming. Of course, I ignored the early red flags, and there were a lot of them. After a short two months together, we decided we should move in together. I thought it was the logical thing to do financially and also romantically – because I thought I was in love with him. Shortly after I paid the damage deposit on our new place (yes, I paid the whole damn thing), he disappeared with my bank card. He was gone for half a day and finally returned it to me while I was at work, because I threatened to get the police involved. He later confessed that he pulled money out to buy drugs, and now was homeless because of a dispute that he got into with his landlord. What a mess. Not even a week later, we were back together. He was so good at making me feel sorry for him and promised it would never happen again. I didn't believe him, but we were to move into our new place a week later and I didn't want to look for a last minute roommate. This situation was only the start of a downward spiral. Five months into our relationship I became pregnant. This kind of news is supposed to make people happy, but I wasn't. I pretended to be happy, but I was more stressed than anything. I began to think long term because I knew I was going to be a single parent.

I was eight weeks pregnant when my daughter's dad first got physical with me. He was in the bathroom and I was going through his phone and saw text messages between him and a friend who sold drugs. He turned it around on me and said I was accusing him of cheating. I was actually accusing him of doing drugs, which he later again confessed to be true. During our confrontation, he wouldn't let me leave our place. He pushed me down when I tried to stand up to leave the room. I was so scared for my unborn child, and began to hyperventilate. I had to lie and say that he could take me to an ATM to withdraw money for him, just to get him to let me out of the house. It was a cold winter night, and I stood by my car waiting for him to find the keys inside. A voice inside my head told me to start walking towards a nearby alley, so I did. He pulled up about 50 yards from the alley and yelled for me to get in the car. The voice told me to run, so I did. I ran to the nearest main street and began to walk as fast as I could to find a phone somewhere. I saw him pulling up around the corner and hid behind a car until he was out of sight. I walked about 10 blocks to the nearest 7-Eleven to call the police. They dropped me off at the local women's shelter, which wasn't the first time I had been there. I remembered being at the same shelter (or one that looked similar), as a child, with my mother. My daughter's dad was in jail for a few days and the police had issued a 'no contact' order.

But we got back together a couple weeks later. This time my excuse was that I didn't want my baby growing up without a dad, like me. I thought he should be given a chance to be a dad. Maybe if he was a good enough dad, it would make up for every time he stressed me out or disrespected me throughout our relationship. We moved back in together, this time in North Battleford, when I was about 6 months pregnant.

Our sweet baby girl, Kalayah, was born on August 9th of that year. I had given birth through a caesarian section and was taking a long time to heal. We didn't get to go home until about 5 days after Kalayah was born. I was left alone most of the time, unable to go to the bathroom by myself because it took three days for me to gain feeling in my legs. I was also breast feeding, and could hardly stand to pick up Kalayah to feed her. I have no idea where her dad was during the day, but thankfully my mom was there to help me half the time. The only time I saw him was in the late evening and morning, while I was in the hospital. I was way too exhausted to ask questions. I lost all of my strength and muscle during pregnancy and child birth and couldn't even lift the car seat to take the baby into the house. After a long 5 days, I was so happy to be home, where I could relax and feed Kalayah.

Having a new baby didn't change anything for my daughter's dad. If anything, his behavior was worse. He was gone all day, and would lie about where he was going. Apparently he was working three jobs (even though I still had to pay most of our bills), and going to the gym in the evenings. He was NEVER home. It didn't really bother me when I was pregnant that he was always gone, because then I could actually relax at home alone. I always had anxiety around him. I never knew when he would have an anger outburst and start throwing things around to scare me. At this point I felt pretty trapped. I had gone back to him twice already after he'd messed up and behaved in a mentally and physically abusive way. I constantly prayed for a way out.

Eight days after giving birth to Kalayah, I had to make an important decision. My daughter's dad had come home drunk, high and angry, because I had threatened to leave him. He immediately picked up Kalayah and began to threaten to kill me, get friends to kill me, and take our daughter away for good. I believed him, and thought I was going to die that night. He began to slap me, punch me and kick me repeatedly until my face was no longer recognizable. He did this while holding our 8 day old baby in his arms. I was completely defenseless, and had given up for a short while. I just lay there, blood streaming down my face, waiting for him to beat me or grab a knife to stab me to death. I prayed hard that my daughter would survive and be well taken care of, far, far away from him. I prayed that someone would hear him shouting and call the police before he dropped her. I prayed that my mom wouldn't show up at my doorstep because she was supposed to come pick us up to go back to the reserve. I prayed for mercy, to the Creator. Not long after I finished praying, I heard a voice inside my head. By this time I was sitting on the couch, waiting for my daughter's dad to tell me what to do. I remembered that he had come in through the living room door, and it was still unlocked. I was ready to jump up, when the voice said "not yet." I waited. He was still holding Kalayah. I didn't want to leave her, but I had to try to run for help. He was pacing around the kitchen, then he went to the bedroom and his back was turned. The voice, even louder now, said "GO!" I ran as fast as my body would allow, to the door, opened it and jumped off the steps. I ran towards the neighbors, barefoot, in the pouring rain and begged them to call the police. The police and ambulance arrived about 20 minutes later. I was relieved that Kalayah was taken from him, unharmed. I had suffered a concussion, and to this day have episodes of short-term memory loss. But things could've gone a lot worse.

My daughter's dad was in jail for just over a week. He was let out on electronic monitoring and was supposed to stay at his stepsister's place in Saskatoon. He sent me over 50 emails while there, going between saying how sorry he was for what he did and that it wasn't right that I was keeping him from Kalayah. One of the last emails he sent stated that he was coming to see the baby. I immediately packed up and left my mom's house, which is where I was living at the time. He had cut off his electronic monitor and was nowhere to be found. I went to stay at a cousin's house for the night. When I arrived at my cousin's, I called my brother crying. I felt desperate to get him put back in jail so I could feel somewhat safe again. I shared my story, a picture of my daughter's dad and a plea for help on Facebook. The post was shared well over five thousand times, but no one knew where he was. I even received a few messages from people questioning my story and some who accused me of seeking attention. After posting my story I went to the local interval house and decided to stay there with my daughter until he was caught. I was filled with anxiety the entire time and never felt safe. I hardly left the interval house during my stay there. A week after my initial post, I shared another picture. This time it was of my beaten face, and next to it, a picture of my daughter's dad. This post got almost 13,000 shares. The next day, he was arrested. He had managed to make it all the way to Calgary, and it was his employer who turned him in. These were the only details I received from victim services, but that information was good enough for me. He was sentenced to a year and a half in jail. I called the correctional facility every few months to make sure he wasn't going to be let out early.

I decided that Kalayah and I deserved happiness, even if it meant that I would be a single mother. I also decided that my daughter's dad wasn't going to have anything to do with us because of his unstable lifestyle, which meant that he was unsafe to be around. My most important decision, however, was to work on myself. I promised myself that I would focus more on my own well-being, so that I could gain back some confidence, be a good role model for other women, and be a great mom to Kalayah.

The first year was incredibly difficult. I felt a lot of anxiety, even though I knew he was locked away. I had recurring nightmares where he would show up at my doorstep, wanting to take Kalayah with him. In my dreams, his eyes looked the same way they did that night, when he could've killed me. I would get depressed thinking about whether or not a man would ever love me or treat me well. I was incredibly self-conscious and didn't like to be out in public because it took a long time for me to shed any of the baby weight. Kalayah would not let me leave her side for the first 6 months. She was also traumatized. I had to carry her most of the day when she was awake. She was also very sensitive to loud noises, so we mostly stayed home. In spite of all that we went through, I am fortunate for the support of my family. I was very fortunate to grow up with a very supportive mother and an older brother who gave me the kind of advice that I wished that I could have got from a father instead. I wouldn't be where I am today if it weren't for their guidance and support, especially after what I had gone through.

I don't regret meeting my daughter's dad, or staying with him for as long as I did. This was by far the most traumatic experience I've had as an adult, but I'm glad it happened. It was my greatest life lesson. After reaching my lowest point in life, I realized that I needed to work on myself. I needed to build up my self-esteem, start playing sports again, get out of my comfort zone and engage in positive self-talk. I am a firm believer in the saying "everything happens for a reason." I looked at my experience as a lesson and tried to figure out what I was to learn from it. I began counselling, once my face healed. I also went to reiki, and participated in Trauma Release Exercises. Playing sports again was a major confidence booster. It took a couple years, but I finally got back in shape and was able to play as well as I did before having Kalayah.

I am constantly searching for ways to better myself and push myself out of my comfort zone, especially this past year. My focus has shifted drastically in the past 5 years, from finding a life partner, to becoming the most positive version of me possible. I used to try to force a relationship to work out. Now I feel that it will happen when it's meant to happen – and with the right person, of course. Since having my daughter, I decided that I want to live a sober lifestyle, so that I can be a good role model for her, like my mother was to me. Recently, I've become a lot more involved in fitness, which I feel may be my calling. A good workout, whether it's sports or the gym, has always been very therapeutic for me."

Kendra has turned her pain into gain. There are thousands of similar stories of people going through pain in their lives. You must be willing to get up and use the pain as fuel towards achieving your goals. This book would not be possible if I hadn't used the pain I experienced in my life: the racism, bullying, loss of a child, and being raised without my dad. This moment between you and I would not be happening right now. Use your pain as fuel towards achieving massive success.

STEP #4: HOW TO GET ANYTHING YOU WANT BY TELLING YOUR STORY

The Power of Your Story

I STARTED OUT this book by telling you my story, because without a story, it is very difficult to understand and trust someone else. The same thing is true with all the opportunities you are going to attract into your life. From interviews, applications, networking, investor meetings, trade shows, speaking engagements and so on, the number one reason people will remember you and want to work with you in the future will weigh heavily on the story you have told.

Now it's your turn to craft your story and use it to get the opportunities that will give you the life you deserve. Here is a simple 3 step method to crafting your story:

1. Find a Turning Point Event (regret, trauma, obstacle, opportunity, etc.)

2. Write It Down and/or Make a Video

3. Share With EVERYONE

It took me nearly a year after launching Neechie Gear to finally share the story of how my friend Johann and his family helped me to take part in soccer when I was an underprivileged youth. One evening, I sat down and began to write down exactly what had happened in my childhood – and how it had empowered me to use my brand to give back a portion of profits to help underprivileged youth who cannot afford to take part in sports. The next step was making a video that showcased the story of what actually happened and the empowering feeling it gave me. The video went viral and our sales increased by 300% over the next 12 months. Without my friend, it wouldn't have been possible for me to play organized sports and ultimately launch my first company years later. It was that turning point event that changed everything. But more importantly, it was the courage to step outside of my comfort zone and share my story with everyone that made the magic happen.

I have had many of my coaching clients follow this process and even share their stories on Facebook, YouTube and in the media. People want to share stories and it is the easiest way to self-market. The experience of sharing your story is uncomfortable if you have never shared anything personal before; but once you do it, you will feel amazing and begin to attract opportunities within your network because you have shared a story – something that most people are too afraid to do. Every entrepreneur I have worked with has seen their sales increase by following this method. Every professional I have coached has seen opportunities come around that they never would have seen had they not shared their story. Your story has the power to help you get anything you want; share it with the world!

How to Influence People with Your Story

When you are meeting new people who have no idea who you are, your story is important. In fact most people are thinking the following things when they first meet you:

1. Who Are You?

2. What Do You Have?

3. Why Should I Care?

Your job is to leave them with a simple pitch that makes them want to ask more questions about you. If you get them asking questions, you have already won. The rest is building more trust and leaving with a call to action that encourages you both to carry on your relationship. The more you make an effort to reach out to the other person, the more the person trusts you and will think of you when opportunities arise.

Here is a pitch I teach our members in the Netmaker Academy. I call it the 6-figure Pitch Formula because my students and I have used it to generate 6-figure sales. You can use this in your life and business. It's very simple and extremely effective to get your point across.

The 6-Figure Pitch Formula

1. Introduction: name, company name and Short Description

2. The Problem: describe the problem you are trying to solve

3. Your Solution: demonstrate how your product/service solves this problem

4. The Close: finish with a call to action that makes them want more!

Pretty simple, right? In 2013, I was competing in a $20,000 business plan/pitch competition in Phoenix, Arizona. For the first pitch, I only had 30 seconds to convince the judges to choose my business to move on to the semi-finals. It was then that I created my pitch off of the above formula. This is what I said:

"Hello. My name is Kendal Netmaker. I am the founder and CEO of Neechie Gear. We are a lifestyle clothing company that empowers youth through sports! We sell everything from men's and women's street and sportswear and at the same time we are committed to providing 5% of our profits to help fund underprivileged youth to take part in sports. You see, when I was in grade 5, my best friend from South Africa helped me to take part in soccer. He and his family paid for my fees, gave me rides to games and eventually gave my family a running vehicle so my mom could continue to drive me to sports. Now fast forward to my last year of university – I was able to create a brand that now impacts thousands of kids across Canada. And now, with over $800,000 in revenue, we are on the brink of exploding!"

Thankfully the judges wanted to hear more and I ended up moving on to the finals and winning the prize money that day. Use the same formula I did and apply it to your life and business to get more opportunities and make prospects want to learn more about you.

If you only have 5 seconds or less in a conversation, you can sum this up by following this script:

I help_____(niche)_____To_____(solve problem)_____ by_____(product/service you offer)_____.

As an example, I would say: "I help driven entrepreneurs and professionals make money with their story through my academy and coaching program!"

If you follow these strategies, you too will see results by influencing the people that cross your path. People only do business with people they know, like and trust. Use the power of your story to create the opportunities that will get you closer to your goals.

STEP #5: THE ULTIMATE SUCCESS FORMULA

THE ULTIMATE SUCCESS Formula was discovered after years of struggling. I got tired of not being able to find a way to be successful faster and I immersed myself in finding out how other successful people were doing it. After discovering the Ultimate Success Formula, my life changed. I went from being a broke university student, struggling to provide for my family, running a failing business and losing thousands of dollars – to completing two degrees, launching several other businesses, winning thousands in business competitions, earning over 25 business industry awards and ultimately creating a life that makes me excited to see each new day! There are three main components to the Ultimate Success Formula and I know that if you implement all three into your life, you will see massive results.

Community of Driven Individuals

You must be around a community of driven individuals who are all trying to get ahead. If you are around toxic and negative individuals, it is going to be very hard to attract the opportunities you want into your life. Here is an example: I recently had a friend who I went to high school with reach out to me on Facebook. He wanted to become successful in his life and wanted me to give him some advice. The first thing I did was check out this dude's Facebook profile. Guess what he was doing? The exact same thing he was doing since we graduated high school; namely, he was partying with the same friends and wondering why his life was not where he expected it to be. If you want to be successful, you are going to have to limit the people you invite into your life, because they can make or break your future opportunities. You must decide and commit to only allowing driven individuals into your inner circle. I learned this the hard way. When I launched Neechie Gear, I wasn't getting the support I expected from some of my friends and family and it inevitably forced me to limit my time with them and find other people to associate myself with. It was difficult for me because some of them were longtime friends or even family members. Soon after surrounding myself with the right people I started attracting opportunities that pulled me closer to my goals.

You see, when you have someone rooting for you and you are rooting for them right back, you start to feed off of each other's energy; you end up helping each other to get ahead much faster than by being on your own. When you have someone who is jealous or negative around you, they can pull you down and keep you living a miserable life like theirs. After coaching dozens of driven individuals over the years, I knew it was time to build the Netmaker Academy and create that same kind of environment where a group of driven entrepreneurs and professionals could come together and support one another to win in life and business.

Access to Information

What goes into your mind becomes your outer world. It is extremely important to carefully monitor what goes into your mind. Everything starts in your mind. If you want to change the way things are in your world, you need to change your thinking; it starts with what goes into our minds. I discovered this in 2014 when I immersed myself in audio programs, books, online courses, documentaries and everything that could help me achieve the goals I had committed myself to. The past year I read over 60 books (and I probably could have read 100 if I wasn't also writing this book). I only read content that I knew would help me achieve my goals faster. Knowledge is power and you can get it from books and from the people you choose to listen to. One of the greatest things you can do today is substitute what you listen to in your vehicle with audio programs that will teach you success strategies to help you in life and business. I started taking what I knew and turning it into video training sessions for people I wanted to help; I then uploaded the sessions to the Netmaker Academy for our members to view them.

One of the hardest things I had to do was substitute TV time with documentaries or video trainings that were going to benefit my future. It's very difficult to try to get ahead if you are in the middle of Netflix marathons or playing video games for hours each day. If you want it bad enough, you will sacrifice these kinds of things in order to obtain the knowledge needed to achieve your goals.

People who are successful strive to find the right information to help them reach their goals and apply the knowledge they have earned toward their success journey.

Mentorship

You cannot achieve your goals without help. Anyone who thinks they can is probably nuts. The biggest secret successful people have is that they have a coach/mentor who helps them achieve their goals faster than other people. In my early years, I had many positive role models who I looked up to – including Johann's father, sports coaches, teachers and family members. A year into my business, I found my first business mentor, Denis Prud'homme, who would be instrumental in holding me accountable and teaching me to do the same for myself. When I said I was going to do something, Denis made sure I did it. Paul Martin would also become another instrumental mentor to me. He would ask me to sit in on TEC Canada mastermind sessions (a program that aims to accelerate the growth and development of Canadian business leaders) with presentations from the top seminar leaders in the world. He would make time for me to grow as an entrepreneur with advice and mentoring along the way. When I wanted to learn and grow in the clothing industry, I paid for consulting from the best in the business, meeting with Daymond John, the founder of FUBU and one of the stars of ABC's Shark Tank. I started to see the value of mentorship and continued to invest in myself. The past year I invested in a coach named Chris Widener. Chris was mentored by Jim Rohn (regarded as one of the most influential thinkers of our time who helped motivate and shape an entire generation of personal-development trainers and hundreds of executives from America's top corporations) for seven years, hosted a show with Zig Ziglar (one of the world's most popular and motivational speakers) and is widely known as one of the top leadership speakers and authors on the globe. That's the power of getting coaching from top people you can find in your network. If you invest in the best there is a high chance you too will become like the best.

Community of Driven Individuals + Access to Information + Mentorship

=

ULTIMATE SUCCESS FORMULA

Keep Moving Forward

In our Plains Cree traditional ceremonies, you will hear elders say "Ahkameyimoh" to encourage participants to keep moving forward, to persist no matter how hard the challenges are. I want you to become who you were born to be and not the person someone else expects you to be. You have everything you need to become successful within yourself. There will always be people who will try to slow you down or discourage you from reaching your goals; it is inevitable. I challenge you to keep moving forward no matter how hard it is or how hard it gets. You must be driven to make your dreams become a reality.

I was told from a young age that everything in life happens for a reason. There is a reason why you and I are here together right now. We have had so many obstacles that we have had to conquer. I've had to battle economic hardship that left me almost ready to file for bankruptcy, the effects of racism, betrayal and losing a child, and so on. Many of these challenges would make most people want to give up on their dreams. But I pushed through these challenges and that has made all the difference. We only grow when we are uncomfortable – and sometimes life forces us to get uncomfortable. But you must see these challenges as opportunities and not problems or setbacks.

There were times when I wanted to react instead of respond. To react is negative, to respond is positive. I was taught by my mom not to engage in conflict because there is no way to win an argument. Throughout my life I faced many negative people. There were many times I was challenged with an aggressive person or situation and wanted to react by getting into arguments and fights – something the person in question was hoping I would resort to. Instead, I did my best to respond by ignoring the person or situation, no matter how much it hurt. When I launched my business, guess who started to buy my products or invite me to speaking engagements? Those same negative people who I had really wanted to fight with in the past. If I had reacted the way they wanted me to in the past, do you think they would have become customers of mine in the future? Likely not.

Forgiveness is a major factor in my own success journey. In order to forgive others, you must forgive yourself. You must know that tomorrow is a new day; you can use it to create a better future for yourself and your family or you can use it to continue doing the same thing you have always done and expect the same results. The choice is yours. I suggest creating a better tomorrow for yourself and your loved ones. You can only get more in your life when you have prepared for a better future in your mind. Your mind is the most valuable asset you can invest in. If you change your thinking, you can change your life and business. Choose to invest in learning that will help propel you closer and closer to your dreams. The more you learn, the more you earn.

Make it part of your mission to serve others. The most successful people are usually the ones who give the most. You can start today by helping others in your life and business.

You must not expect anything in return. I used to think that I would help others only if they would help me in return. I was wrong. I started doing free seminars and mentoring and giving hundreds of hours of free talks to people who needed my guidance. If I was not giving without expecting anything in return, I wouldn't have created another business that focused on helping others achieve their goals. When you give, you receive. I have made it my personal mission to try to give value to everyone I come into contact with. When you genuinely help others, you will receive countless blessings that will come into your life.

If you have struggled since you were young, hang in there, the best is yet to come. The universe has respect for you and something big is waiting for you. But you have to be willing to grind for it. The most successful people in the world have had to overcome major obstacles to get to where they are today. The universe rewards people who work when no one is watching. That is when the true magic happens. Work hard towards your goals and eventually you will find that things will work out in your favor. Too many people look for an easy way out and skip this step. Then they wonder why their lives are not where they expected them to be. There is no way around hard work. Grind day and night and watch the opportunities that you will attract into your life.

You deserve to be successful. Ahkameyimoh, keep moving forward.

ACKNOWLEDGEMENTS

I want to thank all of you who have influenced this book and made it become a reality. Namely: my wife Rachel Netmaker; mom Inez Weenie; my kids; my sisters Kendra, Farrah and Marisha; my friends and inner circle who keep challenging me to think bigger; my relatives who have passed away; my mentors, many of whom have given me countless hours of time; the Strumpher family who helped us when we needed it most; the teachers/coaches/strangers who showed me I had potential when I couldn't see it in myself. Thank you to everyone who has brought me in to speak to your communities and events.

I want to thank the mentors who have helped me whom I haven't met: Zig Ziglar, Les Brown, Tony Robbins, Brian Tracy, Jim Rohn and more.

I want to thank the mentors who have helped me whom I have met: Denis Prud'homme, Paul Martin, Chris Widener and countless others.

Thank you. Ninanaskomon (I am grateful).

Top 10 Books Every Driven Entrepreneur and Professional must read

Think And Grow Rich
by Napoleon Hill

The E-Myth Revisited: Why Most Small Businesses Don't Work and What to Do About It
by Michael E. Gerber

Expert Secrets: The Underground Playbook for Creating a Mass Movement of People Who Will Pay for Your Advice
by Russell Brunson and Robert Kiyosaki

The Alchemist
by Paulo Coelho

Act Like a Success, Think Like a Success: Discovering Your Gift and the Way to Life's Riches
by Steve Harvey

Rich Dad Poor Dad: What the Rich Teach Their Kids About Money That the Poor and Middle Class Do Not!
by Robert T. Kiyosaki

The Monk Who Sold His Ferrari: A Fable About Fulfilling Your Dreams & Reaching Your Destiny
by Robin Sharma

The Compound Effect
by Darren Hardy

The Power of Positive Thinking
by Dr. Norman Vincent Peale

*The ONE Thing: The Surprisingly Simple Truth Behind
Extraordinary Results*
by Gary Keller and Jay Papasan

Top 5 Ways to Make Money Online

1. Teaching Online through webinars

2. Provide a service

3. Create and sell a product

4. Affiliate and network marketing

5. Mastermind/coaching groups

Top Secret Resources for Entrepreneurs & Professionals

Webinars: GoToWebinar.com, webinarjam.com

Landing pages: clickfunnels.com, leadpages.net

Create Membership Sites: clickfunnels.com, wordpress.com, rainmaker.com

Hire Virtual Assistants: upwork.com

Hire Freelancers: fiverr.com, 99designs.com

Sell Products Online: shopify.com

Online Conferencing: skype.com, zoom.com

Email Marketing: mailchimp.com

Online File Sharing/Storage: dropbox.com

Video Hosting: YouTube.com, vimeo.com

Video Editing: iMovie

Online Bookkeeping/Accounting: quickbooks.com

Accept Payments Online/In Person: paypal.com, stripe.com

Social media management: Hootsuite

Buy Audio Programs: Audible app, audiobooks app

**Tell Your Story.
Build Your Brand.
Leverage Your Success.**

KENDAL
NETMAKER

World Class Speaker

Kendal is a Multi-Award Winning Entrepreneur who has been speaking professionally to thousands of people around the globe on motivation, leadership and the power of telling your story.

"… Kendal's keynote was not only touching and motivating, but also funny and light-hearted. Afterwards, you could hear the mumble in the crowd talking and reflecting on all that Kendal had said that touched their hearts and moved them. (He) is a humble and well-rounded human being, We hope to be able to work with him again soon!"

-Martina Sarro, Client Relations Specialist – TEC Canada

**To Book Kendal to Speak at Your Next Event, please visit:
KendalNetmaker.com**